BATTLE FLAGS OF TEXANS

★ ★ IN THE CONFEDERACY ★ ★

ALAN K. SUMRALL

EAKIN PRESS ★ Austin, Texas

FIRST EDITION

Copyright © 1995
By Alan K. Sumrall

Published in the United States of America
By Eakin Press
A Division of Sunbelt Media, Inc.
P.O. Drawer 90159 ★ Austin, Texas 78709-0159

ISBN 0-89015-983-1

10 9 8 7 6 5 4 3 2

Library of Congress Cataloging-in-Publication Data:

Sumrall, Alan K.
    Battle flags of Texans in the Confederacy / written and illustrated by Alan
K. Sumrall. — 1st ed.
        p.   cm.
    Includes bibliographical references and index.
    ISBN 0-89015-983-1 : $29.95
    1. Texas — History — Civil War, 1861–1865 — Flags. 2. United States — His-
tory — Civil War, 1861–1865 — Flags. I. Title.
CR113.5.S86   1994
929.9'2'09764 — dc20   94-40888
                                                                              CIP

For Sam, Carrie, and James.

In memory of
Eldon A. Sumrall, Jr.

How This Book is Organized

The wide diversity of battle flag designs used by Texans in the Confederacy defies any conventional means of organization. Therefore, the flags are shown in a loose chronological format, with considerable and unavoidable overlaps. The organization of the book is intended to give the reader an idea not only of the general evolution of Confederate flag design and usage but also to illustrate the true decentralization of the Confederate military.

Contents

Foreword

In 1967, while I was in graduate school at Louisiana State University, fate would determine that I choose as a research topic for a paper in a "local history" course the Confederate flags of Louisiana's military units during the American Civil War. The paper that resulted formed the basis for a scholarly article that gradually kept expanding until it was published as the 152-page monograph "The Battle Flags of the Confederate Army of Tennessee" (Milwaukee Public Museum, 1976). As originally conceived, the LSU paper was directed at studying the military flags of a single state during the war, without regard to other states. Indeed, the information on what had happened in other states was virtually absent at the time. Only Louisiana, as the result of a 1956 National Guard project to document all of the state's military flags, had a comprehensive body of data on its Confederate military colors. The other Southern states generally had their flags displayed in some central repository, but few had them photographed or had assembled an archive of documentation of the state's flags. Indeed, today only Arkansas and Georgia have pursued the task of gathering the data, photographing the flags, and presenting them in a published form.

Hence, the original paper expanded and developed into the lengthy monograph covering the types of battle flags carried regionally in the Trans-Appalachian theater of operations. This was accomplished only after extensive inductive and archival research with the collections themselves. Had studies such as Mr. Sumrall's been available, the task would have been made infinitely easier. As the research for the 1978 monograph progressed, it soon became evident that the states and their communities were not the only factors influencing the type of flags carried militarily in the South.

Because the National Flag adopted by the Confederacy on March 4, 1861 (the "Stars and Bars") so resembled the flag of the United States of America (the "Stars and Stripes"), the former was hastily discarded as an ineffective military tool. In its place evolved distinctive "battle flags." The battle flag concept, however, did not originate at the national level but within separate regional armies. Thus there were several "battle flags" in use simultaneously.

In Virginia this was the now familiar "Southern Cross," a red field (although in fact most of the earlier ones manufactured were pink for want of scarlet cloth) transversed by a blue saltire (St. Andrew's Cross), usually edged in white and bearing first twelve (in deference to Kentucky's alleged neutrality) and finally thirteen white (but sometimes gold) stars. These flags were usually finished with a border of orange, yellow, or white cloth or a golden fringe.

The flag was initially only used in Virginia, having been designed and adopted by Generals P. G. T. Beauregard and Joseph Johnston after the First Battle of

Manassas (Bull Run). Since there were only three major Texas units serving in that region (the First, the Fourth, and the Fifth Texas Infantry), few Texas units would carry the Army of Northern Virginia patterns of that battle flag.

In the Confederacy to the west of the Appalachian Mountains, other designs were being implemented at about the same time that the Confederate Army of the Potomac (afterwards, the Army of Northern Virginia) was adopting and mass producing its battle flag. In Arkansas, Maj. Gen. Earl Van Dorn, who had experienced the concept of the battle flag while serving in Virginia in 1861, adopted a different design for his "Army of the West" after his transfer to Arkansas in early 1862. This flag also consisted of a red field, but it was studded with thirteen white stars and had a white crescent in the upper, hoist corner. Most of the flags were either bordered or fringed in yellow. Several Texas units, notably the dismounted Third, Sixth, and Ninth Texas Cavalry, received flags of this pattern shortly after the units were transferred with the Army of the West to Mississippi.

Similarly, further up the Mississippi Valley, Episcopal Bishop Leonidas Polk adopted a distinctive battle flag for his forces in Tennessee and neighboring Missouri. This flag had a blue field. Like the Virginia battle flag it was transversed by a cross, but rather than a St. Andrew's Cross, Bishop Polk's battle flag was quartered by the red cross of St. George, also bearing white stars for the number of states considered to have seceded at the time the flag was adopted. Further to the east on the Kentucky line, Simon Bolivar Buckner, senior division commander of Albert Sidney Johnston's "Army of Kentucky," devised another blue battle flag. Buckner's design, however, was much simpler than Polk's and bore a simple white disc in the center of its field, usually inscribed with the unit designation. Later versions incorporated a white border around the edges of the blue field. As the only Texans in those theaters consisted of the Eighth Texas Cavalry, these flags did not see immediate service with Texas commands. However, later in the war, after the exchange of the prisoners captured at Arkansas Post (Fort Hindman), the "full moon" blue battle flags of Hardee's Corps would become dear and tender tokens to the dismounted Texas cavalry and infantry assigned to Cleburne's pugnacious division.

Only the insipid Maj. Gen. Braxton Bragg failed to devise a distinctive battle flag, but his forces would eventually be issued variations of the Virginia flag when Gen. P. G. T. Beauregard was transferred to Mississippi in February of 1862 to serve as Gen. Albert Sidney Johnston's second in command. Like the flags adopted in Virginia, those purchased by Beauregard from New Orleans in early 1862 bore only twelve stars; however, these were heraldically correct six-pointed stars instead of the more common five-pointed stars prevalent in American usage during the nineteenth century. Two Texas units, the Second and Ninth Infantry, would be issued flags of this pattern.

The advent of General Beauregard in Mississippi in early 1862 was the first of several conduits by which the Virginia battle flag design spread westward. Beauregard's second transfer, this time to Charleston in September of 1862, brought forth the design, while its other chief proponent and co-designer, Joseph E. Johnston, brought it back into use, though in a rectangular, borderless, thirteen-star version. Most Texas units were not affected by either transmission of these designs, since no Texas troops served in Beauregard's Department of South Carolina, Georgia, and Florida. Also, by the time Gen. Joe Johnston reinstituted the design in the Army of Tennessee in 1864, all its Texan forces except Douglas' Texas Battery (which eventually did receive the new variant of the battle flag of the Army of Northern Virginia in the size made for artillery batteries) were concentrated in Cleburne's Division. That division successfully petitioned to continue carrying their distinctive blue "full moon" battle flags, receiving at least two new issues of the Hardee-type flag before the end of the conflict.

This is not to say that Texans did not march under the "Southern Cross." Indeed, a good many Texas units that served in the Trans-Mississippi theater carried variations of it. In either late 1863 or early 1864, General Walker's Division, embodying many Texas units, adopted a variation of the design wherein the colors of the field and the cross were reversed. These flags had a blue field with a red St. Andrew's Cross transversing the field and bearing thirteen stars, the central star of which was usually larger. Consistent with other variations (with normal coloration), these battle flags usually lacked the white edging to heraldically separate the color of the field from the color of the blazon (an added device, such as a cross) applied to it. External borders were also usually absent, and the flags were invariably rectangular.

Despite having adopted a new National Flag on May 1, 1863 (the "Stainless Banner," consisting of a white field bearing the Army of Northern Virginia battle flag in its upper, hoist corner as a canton), few Texas units adopted this new flag as a military color. The prominence of the battle flag design as well as the new flag's propensity to be mistaken for a flag of truce or surrender consigned it to relative obscurity. This was a stark contrast to 1861, when the new National Flag adopted on March 4, 1861 (the already mentioned "Stars and Bars") quickly surpassed the readopted 1839 Texas State Flag as the prime military unit flag of Texas commands. That affinity for the "Stars and Bars" would continue in Texas despite the flag's similarity to the U.S. flag. As with battle flags carried by Texas units in the Trans-Mississippi theater, the whim of the maker directed the size and proportions and star patterns of these flags. And, in common with the makers in other states of the Confederacy, that was the rule rather than the exception.

Al Sumrall's comprehensive study of the flags of Texas military units should set a standard for the long overdue studies covering the respective collections of Confederate unit flags in other Southern states. It is hoped that this publication will prompt other authors to follow his lead.

HOWARD MICHAEL MADAUS
Cody, Wyoming
August 1994

A Message to Friends of the Confederacy

The Texas Confederate Museum Collection of the Texas Division United Daughters of the Confederacy is a public trust for the citizens of Texas. As custodians of an approximate two-million-dollar collection of artifacts pertaining to Texas' role in the War Between the States, we have a sincere obligation to the past and present. The most sacred items in this collection are forty original flags, both Confederate and Union.

During the eighty years that the UDC has been the caretaker of this collection, funding has been unavailable to conserve the flags in a permanent manner. Many of these flags, tattered and bloodstained from battle, still smell of smoke and are riddled with bullet holes from 130 years ago. Immediate conservation is needed in order to retain the character of the flags. The UDC flag collection is the most important and complete representation of Texas Confederate history that still exists. Ninety percent of eligible men and boys served the Confederacy, and many of them died under these flags.

The Texas Confederate Museum Collection is fortunate to have formed a fifty-year alliance with Hill College and the Colonel Harold B. Simpson Confederate Research Center in Hillsboro, Texas. The move from our home of eighty years on the Capitol grounds in Austin to Hill College will result in our becoming the largest Civil War museum west of the Mississippi River.

Texas Division United Daughters of the Confederacy is proud to continue working to preserve American history and applauds the completion of books written about the War Between the States. To Alan K. Sumrall we owe a debt of gratitude for his preservation of the history of Texas Confederate battle flags. His paintings of the flags are to be treasured. Without the unselfish dedication of individuals like him, the history and heritage we hold so dear is in danger of being lost forever. Others who have labored to publish this book have the appreciation of all historians.

SHERRY DAVIS, President
Texas Division
United Daughters of the Confederacy

The United Daughters of the Confederacy encourages descendants of Confederate veterans to join our organization. Our objectives are historical, educational, benevolent, memorial, and patriotic. The UDC also encourages the youth of today to join the Children of the Confederacy and men to join Sons of Confederate Veterans.

Donations to help conserve flags in the Texas Confederate Museum Collection may be sent to Treasurer, Texas Division UDC, P.O. Box 30619, Houston, TX 77249-0619.

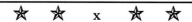

Glossary of Terms

Vexillology is the traditional term used to define the study of flags. Terms used throughout this work are taken from accepted papers and professional publications which are peculiar to this form of study. They are generally military in nature and style. The serious student will do well to become familiar with the vexillological terms used in all books dealing with military heraldry.

GENERAL TERMS

Configuration: The overall shape of the flag, i.e., *rectangular, square, triangular, swallowtail, or pennant.*

Field: The basic colors and design of the flag prior to embellishment with distinctive charges.

Obverse: That face or side of the flag seen when the staff or leading edge (q.v.) is to the viewer's left.

Reverse: That face or side of the flag seen when the staff or leading edge (q.v.) is to the viewer's right.

MEASUREMENTS AND EMBELLISHMENTS

Height on staff (Hoist, sometimes **Width):** The overall vertical distance from the leading edge to the (q.v.) from the uppermost edge to the lowest edge, excluding any fringes but including borders (q.v.).

Distance on fly (Fly, sometimes **Length):** The overall horizontal distance from the leading edge to the most distant point to the fly edge. If the flag is cut swallowtailed, two measurements are required: the first as described above and the second from the leading edge to the cut of the swallowtail nearest the staff.

Border: Material differing in color from that of the field sewn to the exterior edges as binding either as decoration or to prevent excessive fraying.

Fringe: Twisted silk, cotton, wool, or metallic (bullion) fibers, usually binding three exterior edges of the flag and serving the same purpose as the border, although often found on flags with borders.

Leading edge (Heading): A reinforcement, usually differing in material from the field of the flag or the border, sewn to the edge closest to the staff to prevent damage to the field from the stresses of securing the flag to its staff.

Attachments: The means by which the flag is secured to its staff. Three methods predominated during the nineteenth century in fastening military colors to their staffs. The most common attachment was a sleeve, either formed from a separate piece of material sewn along the full length of the leading edge or formed from the body of the field by doubling back the leading edge and sewing it. Pairs of fabric ties, often grosgrain or silk ribbon, sewed to the hemmed leading edge proved least satisfactory in securing the flag, but were nevertheless a common attachment. The least common attachment consisted of whipped eyelets piercing a reinforced leading edge. Through these eyelets, cords, or ties the flag could be fastened to its staff.

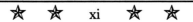

Disc (Sometimes called **"Silver Moon"**): A white oval or circle sewn to the center of the field, as in the Hardee Pattern Battle Flag. When circular, it was measured in terms of its diameter. When oval or rectilinear, it was measured in terms of the major and minor axis, specifying which was horizontal and which was vertical.

Crescent: A "quarter moon" appearing on the field of the Van Dorn Pattern Battle Flag, measured in terms of maximum width and the diameter of a concentric circle.

Cross: A symbol, usually of a color differing from that of the field, set in or across the field. Three basic forms of the cross were used on Confederate flags:

St. Andrew's Cross (in heraldry, a saltire), in which the arms transverse the field diagonally from corner to corner, was most common.

Greek Cross, where the arms were perpendicular to and parallel with the staff, appeared on the Polk Pattern Battle Flag.

Latin Cross, in which the lower, vertical arm has been extended and all arms truncated, appeared on the battle flags of Price's Missouri Divisions.

Fimbriation (Edging, *as contrasted with* **Border):** A thin strip of fabric, usually white, separating an embellishment upon the flag from its field. In heraldry, the fimbriation is used to prevent the false blazonry of applying one tincture directly to another.

Quadrants: Those sections of the field separated by a cross completely transversing a flag. In the case of a St. Andrew's Cross, the quadrants are referred to as staff, upper, lower, and fly. In the case of a Greek Cross, the quadrants are referred to as upper staff, lower staff, upper fly, and lower fly. The upper staff quadrant is similar to the quadrant.

Canton: A square or rectangular piece of cloth, usually contrasting in color to that of the field, and applied to the upper staff corner of the field.

Star(s): Geometric symbols, usually either pentagrams (five-pointed stars) or hexagrams (six-pointed stars) applied to the field or one of its embellishments. As described in the text, the stars are measured across two of their most distant points rather than in terms of the diameter of a concentric circle.

Star separation (when applied to the cross): The distance from the center of the junction of the bars of the cross to the respective centers of the stars upon the arms of that cross.

Battle honors: The names of the engagements in which the unit carrying the flag had participated. These were often hand-lettered or sewn from separately cut letters to the field of the flag.

Unit designation: The name by which the unit was officially designated. In abbreviated form, this designation often appeared affixed to the flag of the unit. Technically, the full unit designation included five basic elements during the Civil War:

1. The seniority number of the unit (or numbers, if more than one had been combined) within the series in which the unit had been authorized and/or the name of the commanding officer.

2. The type of organizational unit (regiment, battalion, company, battery, etc.).

3. The place where the unit originated (the state name, or "Confederate" if from several).

4. The distinction of enlistment (Regular, State Volunteer, Volunteer-P.A.).

5. The branch of service (Artillery — Light or Heavy, Cavalry, Dragoons, Engineers, Infantry, Mounted Rifles, Partisan Rangers, Reserves, Rifles, etc.) or "Legion" if a combined force. Hence the full title of a unit should read, for

instance: *5th Texas Infantry Regiment.* It was common practice in the correspondence of the era to abbreviate many of the unit designations. Frequently titles were shortened to, for example, *5th Texas Infantry* or *5th Texas.* For all infantry regiments, the former abbreviation has been used throughout.

Cross cannons inverted: The barrels of two cannon, crossed and inverted (although frequently displayed muzzles upward) applied to the flag of a Confederate unit of the Army of Tennessee after October of 1862 to honor its capture of Union artillery in combat.

Letter styles: Three types of lettering appear most frequently in the application of unit designations and battle honors on Confederate flags:

Roman style, in which the outer lines of the letters are curved and the width of the component features of the letters varies, is the most common.

Block style, or "plain" letter, was the second most popular, with outer lines curved but component features all of the same width.

Gothic style, similar to the block or plain style, differs in that the outer edges are straight, not curved. Capital (uncial) lettering is most common, but some small (minuscule) lettering is found, especially in the Roman style.

Scales: Most flags illustrated throughout this text were originally drawn and painted to various scales, instead of to a standard scale of, say, ¾ of an inch to the foot. The author-illustrator preferred to work in some cases in actual size renditions so as to more accurately portray the lettering and stars on some flags, and the fabric on others. Measurements are given in the customary system rather than in the metric system because the former was the official system employed during the Civil War.

Confederate Military Organization

Organizational Elements	Commanding Officers
Company (approximately 75 soldiers)	Captain
Regiment (ten to twelve companies)	Colonel
Brigade (three to five regiments)	Brigadier General
Division (three to five brigades)	Major General
Corps (three to five divisions)	Lieutenant General
Army (one or more corps)	General

It should be noted that available troop strengths varied considerably from action to action, due to combat attrition, sickness, and difficulty in obtaining replacements. Independent commands often did not fit into true nineteenth-century military structure. The term "Legion" referred to a regimental-sized unit of mixed infantry and cavalry. The term "Battalion" loosely referred to groups of companies not formally organized into regiments.

The Civil War witnessed the end of massed Napoleonic tactics and saw the advent of defensive "trench" warfare by 1864. This major shift in thinking resulted from the early Industrial Age invention of the rifled musket, which could hit a target at 250 to 1,000 yards. The rifled, automatic machine gun heralded the final demise of massed troop warfare in World War I.

Introduction

During the period 1835 to 1865, the land that is now the state of Texas underwent tumultuous changes. In a scant thirty years, the region changed from a territory of Mexico to the independent Republic of Texas. Then it became a state in the United States of America, seceded to statehood in the Confederate States of America, and finally reverted back to a state in the United States. Three major conflicts—the War for Texas Independence, the Mexican War, and portions of the Civil War (or War Between the States)—occurred within its borders. Each had a major effect on shaping the lives of Texans who survived and impacted the state we know today.

The number of independent flag designs used by Texans was staggering: homemade types for local companies, unique types for belligerent political groups, imported flags for new mercenaries or volunteers, and officially sanctioned flags of government. No single flag existed for the entire period. Only the "Lone Star" symbol showed any type of continuity. After all was settled in 1865, only the Lone Star Flag of Texas (the third flag of the Republic of Texas) survived to continue in government use.

This book is an endeavor to take the reader through a visual foray of discovery concerning the unique heraldry of flags used by Texans in the Confederacy during the war years of 1861–1865. None of the flags illustrated is authentic, as their condition, availability, or absence necessitated. Flags depicted in this work are merely renditions of the originals, created by the author from descriptions of certain flags. Many original Confederate flags can be found in the Texas State Archives at Austin, Texas. Others are in museums, with a few in private collections. A large number of flags are in the custody of the Texas Division of the Daughters of the Confederacy. Many years ago, these flags were displayed in a museum setting. Later they were stored away and are currently unavailable to researchers, historians, and the general public. For many of these flags, not even photographic images are available. They are shrouded in mystery and present a serious challenge to the modern historian. Fortunately, negotiations are being made that may result in the resurfacing of the collection.

In this book, the attempt to capture the images of flags at times comes close to true replication; others only represent the basic design and ambiance of the original. This work is not intended to be the final word in the manufacture of exact replicas. Its purpose is to illustrate what the flags looked like over a century and a quarter ago, when they were relatively new. Time and poor storage have not been kind to most of the surviving originals. In the following pages, the basic patterns and types used by Texas Confederate regiments which served in all theaters of the war are represented. The wealth of original designs is at least hinted at.

For various reasons, not every surviving flag is included. Often one style of flag survives in greater numbers than it does in comparison with other types that might have had a low survival rate. The reader is urged to keep an open mind. Any generalizations about flags of Texas Confederate military units are tentative at best. However, the following discourse is intended to at least make the reader aware that all was not chaos.

Selected Confederate Regimental Pattern Flags

Early Silk ANV*

Cotton Issue ANV
(very limited)

2nd Bunting ANV
(1st Bunting ANV had wider cross)

3rd Bunting ANV

Van Dorn

Department of East Tennessee
(true St. Andrew's Cross)

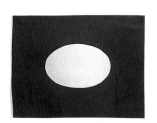

Hardee

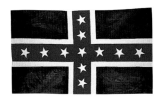

Polk

Bragg

Department of Alabama,
Mississippi, and East Louisiana

Taylor

Johnston

* Army of Northern Virginia and earlier Confederate Army of the Potomac.

Overview of Flag Use in the Confederacy

A brief discussion of flags of the entire Confederate Army is warranted. Afterwards, a summary of possible conclusions concerning Texans' use of these and "home-grown" flags may be helpful to the reader.

The "Bonnie Blue Flag" was a flag associated with the maturing Southern secession movement in 1861. First unveiled as the flag of the very brief Republic of Mississippi, the popularity of the plain blue field with the lone central white star spread like wildfire throughout Texas, Mississippi, and Louisiana, thanks to the song "The Bonnie Blue Flag" introduced by Harry McCarthy, "The Arkansas Comedian." Texas had a long association with the design, and many Texans have strenuously claimed the design as originating with the first Republic of Texas flag in 1836. However, the Bonnie Blue Flag has roots as early as 1810 in Florida.

The newly emergent provisional government of the Confederate States of America, however, had fixed upon a more universal, cohesive style of flag—the "Stars and Bars." Originally raised at the new Confederate capitol at Montgomery, Alabama, on March 4, 1861, the blue square canton, on a field of two red horizontal bars sandwiching a white horizontal bar, contained seven stars in a circle which grew eventually to a total of thirteen. It may have been accidental that this flag was similar to the Federal "Stars and Stripes," but many in the South still carried fond sentiments of the Union.

By then, the "Bonnie Blue Flag" had become a secession relic, a movement which had evolved into fervent nationalism.

Although the Confederacy in 1861 fought battles from Virginia to New Mexico, in June of that year the first major engagement came at Bull Run (First Manassas) in Virginia. In this battle it was noted that the non-uniformly clad Confederate and Union troops (both had regiments wearing blue and gray uniforms) had difficulty in telling friend from foe. The similarity of the flags carried by the troops only added to the confusion.

This learning experience led to the development of a "battle flag" to supersede the Virginia-stationed army's National Flags, along with the various state and/or individualized flags carried by the regiments. At this time, because armies used obsolete Napoleonic battle tactics (obsolete because of the new longer-range rifled musket), flags actually served a vital purpose: to identify unit nationality for field commanders, as well as to prevent accidental or "friendly" fire upon friendly troops. The battle flag also served as a rallying point during the fluid though often chaotic movements of the troops during the cacophony of battle. The flags' visual identification on the battlefield was also a source of security and morale building.

Gen. P. G. T. Beauregard, borrowing from a proposed design that had been rejected as a National Flag in early 1861, proposed a St. Andrew's Cross type of flag of convenient square proportions (a cross of blue on a red field). The original St. Andrew's Cross flag of Scotland has a white cross ("X") on a dark blue field.

Beginning around September of 1861, many twelve-starred silk battle flags were made for as many regiments as possible to this general pattern, their individual sources and details varying. By late 1861, however, it became apparent that silk flags were not sufficient in number or durability. Orders for the army that was

Secession, Confederate National, and Naval Flags

"Bonnie Blue Flag"
The most popular flag of the Southern secession movement

First National Flag
First Naval Ensign
("Stars and Bars")
March 1861–May 1863

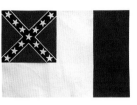

Second National Flag
Second Naval Ensign
("Stainless Banner")
May 1863–March 1865

Third National Flag
April 1865

First Naval Jack
March 1861–May 1863

Second Naval Jack
May 1863–April 1865

A model of the ironclad C.S.S. *Virginia*, displaying the relative positions and sizes of the jack and ensign in Confederate service. The jack was normally used only while the ship was in port. (Model by Al Sumrall)

eventually designated "Army of Northern Virginia" went for a standardized mass-produced battle flag, and the first of seven (possibly eight) types of distinctive issue flags appeared on the line. Their use was overlapped as supply and other factors ruled out complete replacement. The three Texas regiments in that army, the core of Hood's Texas Brigade (several non-Texas regiments/units served in the brigade), would eventually serve under some of these flags.

It was only in Virginia that a large army adopted this centralized method of flag use. By the time the Army of Northern Virginia's battle flag had become commonplace, the main western (but still east of the Mississippi) army, the Confederate Army of the Mississippi (later to achieve immortality as the Army of Tennessee), had solved the problem of the national type misidentification. Their policy allowed corps commanders in the field to choose their own flags for their regiments. This army comprised four corps. Each corps commander had his own ideas as to an appropriate battle flag. General Hardee adopted a blue flag with a white disc in the center. General Polk, Episcopal bishop in peacetime, adopted a blue flag with an upright St. George's Cross of red. The states of the Confederacy were recognized with white stars in the red cross.

The corps under Gen. Braxton Bragg was identified with an exotic square (later oblong rectangular) flag bordered with a wide pink material enclosing a blue St. Andrew's Cross with white fimbriation on a red field. Interestingly, the twelve stars in the cross were *six-pointed*. General Breckenridge, commanding the reserve corps, did not designate a battle flag per se, and stayed with the First National type for his regiments.

Hardee's, Polk's, and Bragg's first issue flags, along with Breckenridge's First National variants, initially flew in battle at Shiloh (Pittsburg Landing), Tennessee. They were probably still in the lesser company of a few state and unique regimental and company flags. The use of the flags (in variant forms) of Hardee, Polk, and Bragg generally stopped after two full years of war. In March 1864, Gen. Joseph E. Johnston, attempting to restore sagging morale, decreed a single battle flag design for the Army of Tennessee. His flag of choice was the thirteen-starred flag we know well today and which is popularly, albeit inaccurately, referred to as the "Confederate Flag" or the "Battle Flag." Of the three original corps flags noted, the Hardee flag has a proven, honored place in the heritage of Texans in the Army of Tennessee, although some Bragg and Polk flags may also have been used by some Texas regiments. Oddly, there is no evidence that any Texas regiment ever used the Johnston flag, so widely recognized today, although other variants of the original square Beauregard battle flag were used. Only one Texas artillery battery might have used the Johnston flag in 1864.

Throughout the Confederacy, departmental and lesser commands chose different kinds of battle flags, many of which would be flown by Texas regiments serving in those units. The situation for Texans serving west of the Mississippi was even more complex and illustrates the western individuality of the Lone Star State. Texans of that era, especially the more youthful ones, dreamed about the prospect of earning glory in war. Volunteers thronged to enlist, many of them worried that the war would be over before they had a chance to fight. Many companies, later to be formed into "Texas" regiments and eventually commanded by Kentucky-born West Pointer Gen. John Bell Hood, made the long trek to Virginia and immortality. They were to become famous as Hood's Texas Brigade.

Regiments such as the Second and Ninth Texas Infantry and the Eighth Texas Cavalry (Terry's Texas Rangers) joined the Army of the Mississippi and fought at Shiloh. They led the way to glory for other Texas regiments to follow in the Central Confederacy. Texas units served at Vicksburg, Mississippi, and most of the major engagements in that region. Other regiments formed and were sent north to Arkansas to protect that state and preserve Missouri for the Confederacy.

The vast lands of West Louisiana, Arkansas, Missouri, Oklahoma (Indian Territory), and Texas would become known as the Trans-Mississippi Department theater of operations, a vital source of supply to the embattled armies of the Eastern Confederacy. This department would see Texans serve the Confederacy in large numbers. In the Trans-Mississippi, Texans would fight in a few fairly large-scale engagements and literally hundreds of skirmishes and other encounters until the end.

Before the cross-Mississippi traffic was closed after the fall of Vicksburg on July 4, 1863, Trans-Mississippi Texas regiments under Gen. Earl Van Dorn had crossed the river in 1862 to fight at Corinth, Mississippi. These forces fought the rest of the war mostly in Mississippi, Alabama, and Georgia under various commands and flags. Other Texas regiments, captured at Fort Hindman (Arkansas Post) in January 1863, were almost immediately exchanged and conveniently handed over to the area where they were most needed: east of the Mississippi.

Hardee's Corps of the Army of Tennessee apparently became the recipient of these Texas "dismounted" cavalry and infantry regiments. (Texas had produced a surplus of cavalry when the real need was for infantry.) Part of Granbury's Texas Brigade, these regiments, although not getting the eastern press coverage that Hood's Texas Brigade enjoyed, fought in some of the most savage and desperate battles of the war. They earned honor after honor and brought glory to their state and their Hardee battle flags.

In the Trans-Mississippi theater, as previously mentioned, Texans chose their own banners. As there was never an official military flag policy in the disorganized and material-poor South, the troops of the Trans-Mississippi became self-supporting. At first, the National Flag or other unique types were prevalent in large numbers, but when news of the war reached Texas, the Beauregard flag (the St. Andrew's Cross) began to gain favor. The process was slow and irregular, certainly not uniform. With the adoption of the Second National Flag of the Confederacy in May 1863 (featuring an Army of Northern Virginia square type flag as the canton on a rectangular white field), the process of Texas units adopting the St. Andrew's Cross battle flags accelerated. However, the Texan flags continued to exhibit great variation in detail.

Apparently, one of the most common characteristics of the Texans' St. Andrew's Cross flags was the deletion or omission of white fimbriation (edging) along the edges of blue cross. Whether this was a practical design reason or whether the first cotton-issue flag of Hood's Texas Brigade in Virginia inspired this practice is unknown. Perhaps it was simply easier to manufacture.

Another common characteristic of many Texas-produced battle flags was a larger star at the center of the cross, a custom first noted with the majority of First National type flags made in Texas. It is possible that when news of the first twelve-starred battle flags was brought to Texas, the center vacancy may have encouraged this practice.

The reader should be cautioned not to generalize too much. There is still a staggering amount of information to be learned about Texans in the Confederacy. The purpose of this book is to inspire interest in the subject of Texas Confederate heraldry, much of which, through our neglect, is disappearing. If a person is fortunate enough to own an original Confederate battle flag, he or she is encouraged to not allow it to become lost to history. The Confederate Research Center at Hill College, Hillsboro, Texas, can at least document the existence of the flag and perhaps someday identify it with a Texas unit, adding a piece to the puzzle of Texas' Civil War history. Its image can then be, once again, part of our Confederate heritage.

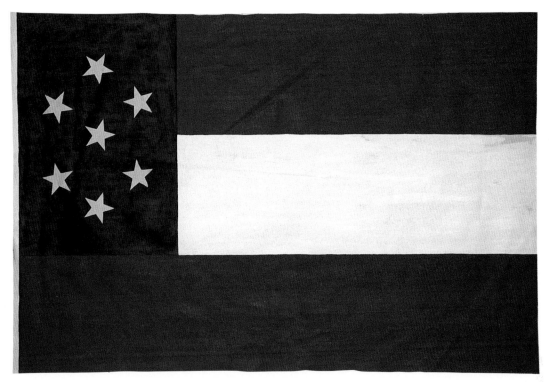

Dimensions: 8½' x 12'

First National Flag Variant

Stars and Bars

Confederate States of America

This very large cotton flag (8½ x 12 feet) is typical of the larger flag used in garrison or civil government service. It is the flag type that first flew in Texas for the Confederate States of America. The centrally located seventh star in the canton was a common local interpretation (not limited to Texas) of the first Confederate States flag raised in Montgomery, Alabama, in March 1861. The provisional congress of the new Confederate States of America had selected a circular pattern of seven stars, and eventually that number increased to thirteen. Most known First National Flags (the true "Stars and Bars") made in Texas featured a central star. The proportions and the blue shade of the canton varied. Many of the early Texas Confederate battle flags were of this pattern, and their service continued long after other theater commanders had chosen other types.

The Confederate States Navy adopted the First National type as its ensign to fly from the sterns of its ships at all times. This flag served until the CS Navy adopted the Second National Flag as its ensign during the summer of 1863. The CS naval vessels serving off the Texas coast probably continued to carry the First National Flag for a considerably longer period as a practical matter. The naval "jack," a flag flown only in harbor at the bow of a ship, was always a rectangular version of the blue canton of the National Flag, a carryover from United States naval practice. This particular First National pattern flag lies folded in a box in the Texas State Archives at Austin, Texas. No state or private funds are presently available to restore or display it.

Dimensions: 31" x 51"

Early First National Variant

Stars and Bars

Wilson County

This 31 x 51-inch variant of the original First National Flag (seven stars) raised at Montgomery, Alabama, is very distinctive with its six-point stars in no real discernible pattern other than the empty center. Both sides of the canton feature seven stars. There is no indication that an eighth star was ever on the flag, and it is possible that the lack of such in the lower right-hand corner was left open for expansion. The number of stars would suggest that the flag was made in the spring or summer of 1861.

This particular "Stars and Bars" reputedly has its origins in Wilson County, Texas, the very place where it resides today in a private collection. It is in reasonably good condition with a tattered fly. Flags of this general size and type would have been in great demand for military use by companies and regiments. In that period Texans would have had no information as to any other Confederate type. However, independent regimental and company types would also see service. This flag was made of silk or a similar material.

Dimensions: 5' x 8' est.

First Texas Infantry Regiment

Lone Star Flag

Hood's Texas Brigade
Longstreet's Corps
Army of Northern Virginia

Carrying a silk Lone Star Flag with painted battle honors, with possibly an early cotton-issue Army of Northern Virginia battle flag, the First Texas Infantry Regiment was almost annihilated in the cornfield at Sharpsburg, Maryland (Antietam) on September 17, 1862.

This unit suffered the highest casualty rate (82%) of any regiment, North or South, in the entire war. The First Texas lost its colors that day in what was arguably the most vicious fighting of the war. Seven color bearers were shot down in succession, along with two officers.

This flag, made by Mrs. Louis T. Wigfall, was first presented to the regiment in 1861 without battle honors.[1] Predating the early silk St. Andrew's Cross battle flags, the First Texas managed to keep this state flag as its regimental colors despite regulations to the contrary. The regiment possibly carried a second regulation battle flag with a second color bearer.

The battle honors would have been applied

during the lull in fighting between the Seven Days and Second Manassas battles in the summer of 1862. When returned to Texas in 1905, only fragments of the white and red bar remained. The existence of the additional battle honors was confirmed as early as November 1862.[2] They were Eltham's Landing and Malvern Hill. By the time the honors were applied, the white color of the star and bar had turned to more of a sand color.

The fringe remnants on this flag today are metallic. It was originally described as silver,[3] although the remaining pieces are gold in color. Possibly the fringe material was silver plated.

The dimensions of the flag, 5 x 8 feet (length estimated),[4] made it one of the largest Confederate battle flags used during the Civil War. This most glorious of all of Texas' Civil War state colors is resting in what may be permanent obscurity. It lies folded in a box at the Texas State Archives, awaiting funding for restoration.

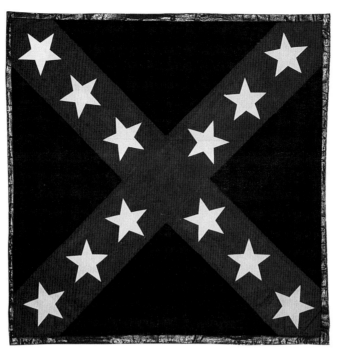

Dimensions: 3½' x 3½' square approx.

First Texas Infantry Regiment

Cotton Issue

Richmond Clothing Depot
Army of Northern Virginia

Found by Union troops with the First Texas' Lone Star Flag at the Sharpsburg (Antietam) battlefield in 1862, this color was a limited issue given only to regiments in two or three brigades in Lee's Army of Northern Virginia. Regiments in Hood's Texas Brigade were among the recipients. The cotton issue type was intended to replace state and silk battle flags, but as will be seen, actual use of particular battle flag types was both confusing and contradictory until the dominance of the prolific white-bordered Third Bunting Issue battle flag by the summer of 1863.

Even after the use of the Third Bunting Issue became widespread in Lee's army, isolated earlier examples of this and other battle flags would crop up in engagements, possibly having been kept as spares by frugal regimental adjutants, while others were either used until worn out or lost. One example of this illustrated cotton issue type was captured at the Battle of the Wilderness from a non-Texas unit as late as May 1864.

While no other flag of this type has been known to survive and have been documented with the other Texas regiments in the Texas Brigade, another identical flag of a non-Texas regiment in the brigade has. The Eighteenth Georgia Infantry served in the brigade until replaced by the Third Arkansas Infantry after Sharpsburg in November 1862. The Eighteenth used the same type cotton issue flag as the type illustrated here. The flag survives today, a tear repaired with a woven lock of hair from a Union Zuave killed during the Battle of Second Manassas.

The cotton issue featured twelve fairly large white stars on a medium blue or possibly light blue St. Andrew's Cross (now faded to light green). It was bordered with an orange-colored tape to prevent fraying.

This flag needs professional restoration care at the Texas State Archives.

*Lt. **B. F. Price**, K Company, First Texas Infantry Regiment (Mrs. C. B. Williams; courtesy Colonel Harold B. Simpson Confederate Research Center, Hill College)*

*Cpl. **Howard E. Perry**, Company H, First Texas Infantry Regiment. Killed at Sharpsburg, Maryland. (Courtesy Colonel Harold B. Simpson Confederate Research Center, Hill College)*

*Pvt. **John Beverly Henderson**, Company D, First Texas Infantry Regiment. (Courtesy Colonel Harold B. Simpson Confederate Research Center, Hill College)*

Dimensions: unknown — 7" x 13" approx.

First Texas Infantry Regiment

Streamer Flag

Hood's Texas Brigade
Longstreet's Corps
Army of Northern Virginia

George A. Branard, the primary color bearer of the First Texas Infantry Regiment, reputedly flew this little flag on the staff above the regimental colors. In the hospital at the time of Sharpsburg, Branard did not carry the colors that day and apparently retained this small flag, which permitted its subsequent use. Made in Houston, Texas, and presented to him by six young ladies, the flag may have been intended to recognize the Lone Star of the Texas State Flag along with the bars of the First National Flag.

At the Texas State Archives is an oblong flag of the same general design (seized from a suspected British blockade runner off the Carolina coast). Another flag of more uniform dimensions at the State Archives is probably associated with a Texas unit. At least one Virginia regiment used this type flag early in the war.

Recently, a flag of this type with the designation *"4th Texas Infantry Regiment"* placed in the canton of the flag surfaced in a private collection. Unfortunately, it has been exposed as an outright fake or an original flag from a real regiment with faked Texas unit designation to make it more marketable. Fortunately, much of Texas' Civil War flag heritage has already been documented by the Texas Division of the United Daughters of the Confederacy, as well as scholars and experts.

Although undiscovered or previously unknown flags do appear occasionally, the increasing demand from both domestic and foreign collectors has created an opportunity for criminals to bilk the unwary.

George A. Branard
(Courtesy Colonel Harold B. Simpson Confederate Research Center, Hill College)

Dimensions: 16" x 34"

Fourth Texas Infantry Regiment

Company B

Hood's Texas Brigade
Army of Northern Virginia

This small, 16 x 34-inch flag has been attributed by the United Daughters of the Confederacy–Texas to Company B, Fourth Texas Infantry Regiment, Hood's Texas Brigade of the Army of Northern Virginia. Although it is certainly too small to have been used as a regimental standard, it was quite possibly used as a camp flag. However, small flags often served as infantry flank markers in combat. The latter were small enough so as not to be confused with the larger battle flags. In some instances, smaller flags may have served as battle flags.

The flag rests today in the care of the Confederate Texas Museum, United Daughters of the Confederacy–Texas Division. Like many of the flags of the Civil War era, it is in sore need of funds for preservation and repair.

Another flag of similar size has been attributed to the First Texas Infantry Regiment. It is in such deteriorated condition that very little can be said about it. All that remains is what may appear to be beige material (faded silk) and remnants of an apparent red star. It should be stated here that the flag may or may not have been a Texas State Flag, but many small flags of various designs saw service on both sides.

Dimensions: 46" x 44"

Fourth Texas Volunteer Infantry

Company D

Hood's Texas Brigade
Army of Northern Virginia

Capt. Alonzo Millett received this striking flag from the ladies of San Antonio in 1861, and presumably took it with the company when it went to Virginia. The motto on the flag certainly attests to the new nationalist feeling circulating through the South at the time. However, it is coincidentally representative of the true St. Andrew's Cross of Scotland symbol, a white cross on a blue field. The reason for the triangular symbols is unknown.

Although it is unconfirmed if this early flag saw combat, the white cross and blue field flag design did see some use as an official battle flag. Gen. Kirby Smith, while commanding the De-partment of East Tennessee in 1862, adopted this type of flag for units in his command. Several examples of these Confederate regimental colors have survived, courtesy of the fact that they were captured in action by Federal forces.

This flag measures 46 x 44 inches, exclusive of the white fringe and red border, and has eleven eyelets along the hoist edge for attachment. The material used was silk, although the fringe was wool.[5]

The flag rests in the care of the Texas Confederate Museum, United Daughters of the Confederacy–Texas Division.

Dimensions: 4' x 6' approx.

Fourth Texas Infantry Regiment

Company K

Hood's Texas Brigade
Longstreet's Corps
Army of Northern Virginia

This flag is an excellent example of First National variants made in Texas and used in large numbers early in the war. The rallying cry "VICTORY OR DEATH" is its most noteworthy asset. The flag was in Athens, Texas, in 1940 in private hands and may still be there.[6]

This flag was mentioned to have been made for and carried by the men of Company K from Harrison County, Texas, and was presented to the company on May 18, 1861.[7] Mrs. Jurusha Walker and Mrs. Dull Averiett are credited with making the flag. At this stage of the war, almost all flags were made by local women to very vague specifications.

The practice of including a larger central star in Texas-produced National Flags was probably not officially specified, although it may have been for battle flag use. More likely, the intensely patriotic Texas women across the region could not resist giving Texas-produced flags some special recognition.

The flag was probably carried to Virginia and later retired from service when orders were issued for all regiments in the Army of Northern Virginia to utilize the square St. Andrew's Cross type battle flag. The use of large flags by independent infantry companies had a tendency to

fade out as the war wore on. Companies starting out at full strength in the beginning often became mere shadows of themselves through combat attrition and illness. This was especially true of troops serving east of the Mississippi, and their individual identities were diminished accordingly.

The actual size of this flag is unknown; 4 x 6 feet seems a reasonable estimate given the averages for flags of this type.

3rd Lt. Wm. D. Ronnsavall, *Company K, Fourth Texas Infantry Regiment. (Courtesy Colonel Harold B. Simpson Confederate Research Center, Hill College)*

Dimensions: 4' x 4' square approx.

Fourth and Fifth Texas Infantry Regiments

Early Silk Flag

Hood's Texas Brigade
Longstreet's Corps
Army of Northern Virginia

Two flags of the Army of Northern Virginia's early battle flag specifications were made from the silk wedding dress of the wife of the Texas Brigade's first commander, Brig. Gen. Louis T. Wigfall, by their daughters, Fannie and Louise.[8] The flag was presented to the Fourth Texas Infantry Regiment while the brigade wintered at Dumfries, Virginia.[9] About the same time, in January 1862, the sister flag, presumably similar, was presented to the Fifth Texas Infantry Regiment.[10] These flags were made in Virginia. Probably a pale red at first, the red dye faded rapidly. The presumed similar flag of the Fifth Texas was retired near the end of 1862. It last saw action during the Seven Days battles.

The illustrated Fourth Texas' flag lasted until October of 1862. Suffering severe battle damage at Antietam (Sharpsburg), Maryland, it was returned to Texas shortly thereafter. From 1865 to 1871, it lay buried in the bank of Barton's Creek to hide it from Union occupying troops. Upon exhumation, it became a common sight at Fourth Texas reunions.

This flag measures about 4 x4 feet.[11] When it was retired, sixty-five bullet holes and three tears from artillery shell fragments were counted.

Due to a misrepresentation on a painting, one publication has depicted it having a white field with red outlines of the St. Andrew's Cross and red stars on a white cross. This is erroneous.

Although history has bequeathed the sobriquet "Hood's Texas Brigade" to the Texans in Lee's Army of Northern Virginia, General Hood only commanded the brigade a short time, as he quickly rose to divisional command. There never was a Hood's Texas Division, although Hood commanded the division of which the Texas Brigade was a part until after the Battle of Chickamauga in late 1863. It is not well known that non-Texan units rounded out the strength of the predominantly Texan-manned brigade.

The flag rests in the care of the United Daughters of the Confederacy–Texas Division, in need of funds for preservation.

Dimensions: unknown — 5' x 8' est.

Fifth Texas Infantry Regiment

Lone Star Flag

Hood's Texas Brigade
Longstreet's Corps
Army of Northern Virginia

According to the records of Campbell Wood, adjutant of the Fifth Texas through the Battle of Gettysburg, the officers of the Fifth Texas at their own expense had a silk Lone Star Flag with silver fringe made in Richmond.[12] It may have been similar to the First Texas Infantry flag. Unfortunately, they were advised that they would not be permitted to use it because of recent orders prohibiting the use of state-type regimental flags. This was somewhat contradictory when one considers that the First Texas was permitted to use its old Lone Star Flag as its regimental colors.[13] It is possible that the First Texas was allowed to use the old flag until it was worn out. Another possibility is that the regimental flag may have been carried with the cotton-issue battle flag. Another explanation might be that no one had complained of the First Texas' use of its Lone Star Flag.

Between the Seven Days battles and Second Manassas campaign in the summer of 1862, the regiment was presented a new cotton St. Andrew's Cross battle flag, a Texas-made replacement for the regiment's already worn-out silk Wigfall-made battle flag. Immediately the new battle flag was called in by divisional headquarters in order that battle honors could be painted on it.

According to Wood, Capt. J. S. Cleveland suggested a subterfuge be attempted. Wood, as adjutant and therefore in charge of the regimental colors, responded that if the St. Andrew's Cross regimental flag was returned from divisional headquarters to his office desk while he was absent, and if it was subsequently spirited away by an "unknown person" (Captain Cleveland), then he (Wood) could disavow any knowledge of the flag being returned. The Texas State Flag could then be justified as a temporary substitute.

Confident of the flag's timely disappearance, Wood quietly secured the Lone Star Flag and had it furled on the staff and ready when, on the very next day, the regiment began the march for what was to be the Second Manassas

Campaign. Furled, the distinctive Lone Star Flag went unnoticed and was assumed to be the regulation regimental color.

Later that day, Gen. John B. Hood, the division commander, ordered a divisional review. This necessitated the unfurling of regimental flags. As he passed down the line, Hood, alert as usual, noticed that the Fifth Texas had "neglected" to unfurl its flag. Hood stopped and asked the obvious question. He was answered by the unfurling of the unauthorized Lone Star Flag.

A cheer broke loose in the ranks as the Texas State Flag was seen. After he had heard Wood's lame white-lie, Hood, whose grim countenance is legendary, reportedly smiled. He then let Wood know that he suspected trickery but promptly left the flag with the regiment.[14]

This Lone Star Flag, apparently alone, was flown by the Fifth Texas at Second Manassas and at Sharpsburg. Severely battle-damaged, it was retired and sent home,[15] presumably heralding the "finding" of the Fifth's St. Andrew's Cross flag. The Lone Star Flag was allegedly destroyed by burning in 1865, perhaps to prevent it from falling into Federal hands.[16]

The accompanying illustration is a depiction of how the flag may have looked. It appears that many state flags used by Texas units may have made "tilted" stars the rule rather than the exception.

Also of note is the silver fringe, which was actually described to be on this particular flag and which is similar to the regimental color of the First Texas' Lone Star Flag.

The battle use of Lone Star Flags with the Texas Brigade did not end at Sharpsburg. There is an account of another Lone Star Flag made by Mrs. Wigfall to replace the lost flag of the First Texas in the cornfield at Sharpsburg. It was bordered in black crepe as a memorial to those Texans already fallen. No longer permitted to be used as the regimental color, it was nonetheless used with what probably was a Third Bunting Issue flag at Gettysburg, Pennsylvania, in July 1863.[17] Further use of a Lone Star Flag after 1862 by the Fifth Texas is not known at this time, but was probably unlikely.

Sgt. Hugh Dickson Boozer
Company G, Fourth Texas Infantry Regiment

Flag Dimensions: 37" x 42" approx.
Streamer Dimensions: 4" x 57" approx.

Fifth Texas Infantry Regiment

Battle Flag and Streamer

Hood's Texas Brigade
Longstreet's Corps
Army of Northern Virginia

This flag of the Fifth Texas raises as many questions as it may answer. Circumstantial evidence would indicate that this cotton flag was made by a Texan, Mary Young, and presented to the regiment around June 1862.[18] The illustrated flag exhibits a large central star and lack of a white edging on the St. Andrew's Cross. These characteristics were common but not necessarily exclusive for Texas-made flags. It may be the same flag temporarily "lost" by the regiment to allow for its flying of the silk Lone Star Flag at the Battles of Second Manassas and Sharpsburg.[19]

After the Fifth's silk Lone Star Flag was prematurely retired due to severe damage following the Sharpsburg battle, this regimental color presumably reappeared and saw service from October 1862 into Lee's Wilderness Campaign in the spring of 1864.

A postwar photograph indicates that in July 1862 at least three battle honors were applied to the obverse side of the flag (one side only, the accepted practice).[20] It is highly possible that the flag had four honors originally, the "Seven Pines" honor having been worn off in service. The illustration addresses this possibility, based upon the nearly identical honors of a non-Texan Army of Northern Virginia regimental flag of the same time period (Eleventh Mississippi).

A white (with dark blue or black Roman numerals and letters) regimental designator was placed upon it and a battle streamer (both sides illustrated) accompanied the flag during all or part of its career.

One of the most famous incidents of the Civil War involved this flag and streamer. At one crucial point in the Wilderness Campaign, Lee attempted to personally lead the Texas Brigade. Cries of "Lee to the rear!" by the Texas and Arkansas troops to their beloved leader and the checking of Lee's horse by one of the Texans inspired several paintings in which this flag and streamer play a central role.

The worn-out and battle-damaged flag and streamer survive in storage today at the Texas State Archives.

A square, white-bordered Richmond Depot bunting issue (probably one of the last Third Bunting Issues) may have become the regimental standard after the Wilderness Campaign. However, there is speculation that another flag was sent from Texas.

Dimensions: 4' x 4' approx.

Third Bunting Issue

Richmond Clothing Depot
Army of Northern Virginia

This battle flag pattern began to be used just prior to the summer actions of 1862. Although the actual Third Bunting type has not been confirmed with a Texas regiment, its use in Hood's Texas Brigade (with the possible exception of the Fifth Texas) is highly probable. Made of wool bunting, the type varied in size for infantry, artillery, and cavalry. Infantry flags normally measured approximately 4 x 4 feet.

The Third Arkansas Infantry, a member of the Texas Brigade after Sharpsburg and remaining with the brigade for the rest of the war, was presented a flag made in Fredericksburg, Virginia in the winter of 1862–63. This flag was identical to the Third Bunting Issue. Oddly, a regimental designator for the Arkansas unit (similar to that used by Fifth Texas on its "Young" battle flag) was placed over the center star on the obverse side only, along the blue cross.

Beginning in June of 1864, the Richmond Clothing Depot began issuing variations of this type, for the most part being increased size,

spacing of the stars, and some differences in the width of the blue St. Andrew's Cross. The Fifth Texas possibly received one of these later types when they retired their Texas-made battle flag after the Wilderness Campaign. It is more likely that the First and Fourth Texas Regiments received this type of flag after Sharpsburg. Unfortunately, the Texas Brigade's headquarters burned in Richmond, possibly with many items, including flags, that would be treasures today.

A large, twelve-starred, white-bordered later bunting issue from the Richmond Clothing Depot was lost by the First Texas Infantry Regiment near Appomattox in April 1865. General Beauregard, placed in command of the military department dominating the Atlantic Coast, also adopted this general type for his regiments in 1862–63.

At least one Texas non-Army of Northern Virginia brigade (Ector's) would fly a late war variant of this square, white-bordered flag in the defense of Mobile in 1865.

Dimensions: unknown — possibly 5' x 8'

First Texas Infantry Regiment

Second Wigfall Lone Star Flag – Gettysburg

Army of Northern Virginia

On the second day of Gettysburg, the Texas Brigade under Robertson, as part of Hood's Division on the Confederate right, advanced upon the general area of "Devil's Den" and "Little Round Top." The Fourth and Fifth Texas Infantry attacked Little Round Top in conjunction with the Alabamans of Law on their right. However, the First Texas and Third Arkansas Infantry, the other half of the Texas Brigade, wheeled to their left in the Devil's Den area. All four regiments fought fiercely against Union regiments that matched their desperation and courage. In the end, it was the unfavorable terrain (for attack) that gave the Federal troops the edge they needed to barely hold, even though the Confederates did make slight gains.

The Fifth Texas carried the cotton battle flag sent from home and adorned with battle honors. It is possible that the blue streamer was carried at that time also. The Fourth Texas presumably carried a white-bordered Third

Bunting Issue. The First Texas probably carried a Third Bunting Issue battle flag as its official regimental flag, but there is evidence that the First Texas unofficially retained a replacement silk Lone Star Flag made by Mrs. Louis T. Wigfall to replace the Lone Star colors lost at Sharpsburg (Antietam).

The flag had special significance. Reputedly, it was edged in black crepe as a memorial to the many dead of the regiment. The flag, according to veteran Samuel R. Burroughs and noted by Howard Madaus in "The Southern Cross," apparently saw action at Gettysburg, unfurled against standing orders and used by the flag bearer in place of the battle flag in a charge against an exposed Union battery. That incident has been portrayed in an inspiring painting by artist Dale Gallon of Gettysburg, Pennsylvania. However, the Lone Star Flag depicted has a yellow or gold fringe and appears more squarish in proportion than one would probably expect.

The star is also upright. If Mrs. Wigfall followed the same pattern she used on the "first" First Texas flag, one would expect the star to be tilted. The black crepe border could have been a logical memorial considering the near annihilation of the First Texas at Sharpsburg.

The length of the flag is speculative. However, the mere shreds of the surviving Sharpsburg flag do not justify the assumption that the Sharpsburg flag was square. The black and white photo of the First Texas flag in the Texas State Archives does not differentiate between supportive backing and the actual remaining white and red bars. Texas flags were normally more rectangular in porportion, although at least one, captured at Port Hudson, Louisiana, was of a more square appearance.

The illustration can only be presented as an approximation of how the "Second Wigfall Lone Star Flag" might have looked. The presentation is justified as a memorial to the fallen soldiers from Texas as well as perhaps the last battle use of the Lone Star Flag. It is highly likely that use of the Lone Star Flag by the Texas Brigade in Virginia was curtailed more by circumstances of the war rather than by any official decree.

DATES OF SECESSION OF THE SOUTHERN STATES

	Seceded
South Carolina	December 20, 1860
Mississippi	January 9, 1861
Alabama	January 11, 1861
Florida	January 11, 1861
Georgia	January 19, 1861
Louisiana	January 26, 1861
Texas	February 1, 1861
Virginia	April 17, 1861
Arkansas	May 6, 1861
Tennessee	May 6, 1861
North Carolina	May 13, 1861
Missouri (secession debatable)	October 31, 1861
Kentucky (secession debatable)	November 18, 1861

Dimensions: 3½' x 7'

Third Texas Volunteer Cavalry

Tyler Guards

Prewar Origin

Colorful and large, this 3½ x 7-foot silk swallowtail flag may have been the first regimental color of the newly formed Third Texas Volunteer Cavalry. Made in 1858 by Mrs. John Robertson, Mrs. George Bates, and Mrs. George Chilton for local militia use, it was originally presented to George Chilton.

When formed in June 1861, the Third Texas was also referred to as the "South Texas-Kansas Regiment," perhaps alluding to the expected theater of operations. While indeed serving in this region initially, the Third Texas Cavalry would later be part of Texas' contribution to the Confederate forces east of the Mississippi, becoming part of Ross' Texas Cavalry Brigade.

This active regiment fought under several types of battle flags in its career, several of which are included in this text. It is unconfirmed if this flag was used at the first significant battle in which the regiment was involved (Wilson's Creek, Oak Hill, Missouri).

In the early stages of the war a relatively large quantity of flags were available, and regiments could have used several flags in combination. It is also possible that this flag would have been too impractical for extended use as a battle flag. It bore far too much resemblance to the "Stars and Stripes" of the Union Army, perhaps even more so than the Confederate "Stars and Bars."

This flag resides with the Smith County Historical Society, Tyler, Texas.[21] Sources indicate that the yellow portions were originally gold-colored. Today the flag exhibits a cream color in place of white (as shown) as well as a light gray color to the pink area shown. Additionally, traces of white markings remain, probably from an inscription surrounding the ring. The fringe appears to have been possibly gold-colored.

This flag is the only known flag honoring the Knights of the Golden Circle, a Masonic organization.

Dimensions: 34" x 42"

Twelfth Texas Cavalry Regiment

Parson's Dragoons

The Twelfth Texas Cavalry Regiment, often referred to as "Parson's Dragoons," received a flag made in the Houston, Texas, vicinity on December 29, 1861, and based on the "Beauregard Battle Flag." The Twelfth Texas Cavalry, formerly the Fourth Texas Cavalry, under Col. William Parsons, was eventually combined with two other Texas regiments (one being the Nineteenth Texas Cavalry), to form Parson's Texas Cavalry Brigade. The regiment served in the Trans-Mississippi theater for the duration of the war and saw action in Missouri, Western Louisiana, and Arkansas.

The illustrated color, possibly the aforementioned Beauregard flag or a later regimental or even a company flag, features common "Texas-made" characteristics in that it lacks the white fimbriation or edging on the blue St. Andrew's Cross but includes a large, central star. The flag measures 34 x 42 inches.[22]

It is possible that this flag associated with Company K of the regiment.[23] Early in the war, the use of company flags was very popular.

The Parson's Flag is on display at the Colonel Harold B. Simpson Confederate Research Center, Hill College, Hillsboro, Texas.

Dimensions: 4½' x 6'

Unidentified Texas Confederate Unit Flag

Red Star

The dominant, five-pointed red star in this flag may be unique for a Confederate battle flag. Of particular note is the shield "TEXAS" painted in red-shadowed brown lettering, and the yellow star on the white bar. Eleven white stars adorn the red star, indicating 1861 issue. There has been a suggestion that this flag might have been associated with a unit called the Fifth Texas Volunteer Cavalry, an early Confederate regiment.[24]

The red star on this illustrated flag may have been included to recognize the Native American contribution to the Confederate cause. Five Native American nations (Cherokee, Chickasaw, Choctaw, Creek, and Seminole) formally allied themselves with the Confederate States of America. From the piney woods of East Texas, individual Alabama-Coushatta braves joined the companies that were to become Hood's Texas Brigade. They fought integrated in the ranks of the Army of Northern Virginia.

The historical value of relics such as this flag becomes apparent when viewing them stimulates conjecture and research.

The flag is one of many resting in boxes in the Texas State Archives.

Dimensions: 3' x 6½'

Tenth Texas Cavalry Regiment

First National Variant

One unit color unquestionably demonstrated the Native American commitment to the cause of the Confederacy: the Tenth Texas Cavalry. The flag of this unit exhibits not only the eleven stars of the Confederate States as they existed when the flag was made, but also four of the Native American nations. The rectangular canton of this cotton flag is unusual, but its dimensions (3 x 6½ feet) are not.

This flag is in the collection of the Texas National Guard Museum at Camp Mabry, Austin, Texas. It was probably used in the early operations of the unit west of the Mississippi. In the spring of 1862 the Tenth Texas Cavalry was ordered across the Mississippi and served primarily in an infantry (dismounted cavalry) capacity. It fought in the Battles of Corinth, Stone's River, Chickamauga, Missionary Ridge, and the Atlanta Campaign, as well as numerous other actions.

The Tenth Texas Cavalry served in Ector's Texas Brigade and most probably used several different types of battle flags throughout its career in the Confederate Army.

Dimensions: 3' x 6½'

Tenth Texas Cavalry Regiment

Company E – "Bully Rocks"

If every company in the Tenth Texas Cavalry had large, cotton, 3 x 6½-foot flags such as the illustrated one, the sight of this regiment on parade must have been colorful indeed. Most companies in Confederate units gave themselves fanciful names. The white "bar" in the early "Stars and Bars" pattern was a convenient and striking location for unit names or inspiring slogans. "Warren Guards" and "Wilson Guards" were other First National types used by companies who identified themselves by names on the white bar.

Unlike the First National Flag of this regiment, this company banner more closely follows the standard "Stars and Bars" specifications in that it has a square canton. Like the majority of Texas' First National types, it features a large, central star.

This flag is at the Texas National Guard Museum, Camp Mabry, Austin, Texas.

Dimensions: 3' x 7' approx.

Fifteenth Texas Volunteer Infantry Regiment

Company D

Reputedly made by the women of Tyler, Texas, and presented to Company D, Fifteenth Texas Infantry on October 14, 1861, this eleven-starred flag with gold metallic fringe measured approximately 3 x 7 feet.[25] It had a rectangular canton. The white bar was made from a flour sack, while the white border (applied to the top and hoist edges only) was of silk.

The remainder of the flag was a wool-cotton mix. The pattern of the stars was elliptical rather than the standard circular.

The Fifteenth Texas Infantry was primarily composed of troops from Speight's First Texas Infantry Battalion. It should not be confused with Ashley Spaight's Eleventh Texas unit.

The Fifteenth served in the Trans-Mississippi theater.

Dimensions: 4½' x 6½'

First National Variant

Lone Star

Unidentified Unit

Although the practice of placing a single star in the blue canton was not common, these type flags have not been noted as an exclusively Texas type. Little is known of this particular flag.

An unconfirmed photograph indicates the possibility that the Thirteenth Texas Cavalry carried a flag of this type, possibly late into the war at Mansfield. The purported flag of the Thirteenth had a designation or slogan on the white bar.

This flag was expensive, as it is made of silk and features stiff metallic wire fringe. The fringe may have been gold-colored or gilt. Note the tilted star.

The flag lies unrestored at the Texas State Archives. It measures 4½ x 6½ feet.

Dimensions: 31" x 72"

Third Texas Volunteer Cavalry

Company K

This oblong, 31 x 72-inch color was possibly used as a regimental flag of the Third Texas Volunteer Cavalry Regiment.[26] It may have replaced or was used with the more fanciful but impractical "Tyler Guards" flag. It reputedly saw action at Oak Hill, Missouri, Elk Horn (Pea Ridge), Arkansas, and Farmington, Mississippi. The flag was retired and sent home after this last action in 1862. It may have been retired in favor of a twelve-starred St. Andrew's Cross battle flag similar to the Army of Northern Virginia's early silk type, or more likely a red battle flag with a red field, white crescent moon, and thirteen white stars of the Van Dorn Pattern Flag, fea-

tured later in this text. Both type flags may have been used in this 1862–63 period of the war.

The Third Texas Cavalry, along with the Sixth, Ninth, and Twenty-seventh Texas cavalry regiments, eventually became known as Ross' Cavalry Brigade. The unit fought mounted in operations in the Central Confederacy until the end of the war.

The illustrated color was made of silk. The stars of this particular flag were silver-colored (a not too common practice) and were placed in an oval pattern.

This rare flag survives today in the care of the Smith County Historical Society, Tyler, Texas.

Dimensions: 42" x 45"

Seventeenth Texas Infantry Regiment

Trans-Mississippi Theater

The Seventeenth Texas Infantry Regiment served its entire career in the Trans-Mississippi Department. It should not be confused with the Seventeenth Dismounted Cavalry, elements of which saw service on both sides of the Mississippi.

All of the engagements of the Seventeenth Texas were in Arkansas and Louisiana. It saw action in twenty-six different engagements, including Sabine Cross Roads, Pleasant Hill, and Mansfield. As a part of Gen. Richard Taylor's army in 1864, it probably flew a red cross/blue field flag.[27] However, it apparently received the flag depicted here earlier in its career.

The flag is 42 x 45 inches and is a cotton issue similar to a flag of the Sixth Texas Infantry Regiment, featured later in this text. It is not yet known if the similarity is merely coincidental. Only if other flags of similar design appear can any conclusions be made as to whether this flag was part of a specific pattern design.

The flag apparently saw significant action. William Westmoreland of Company E reputedly saved it after the color bearer was shot down. The flag now resides in the care of the Harrison County Museum, Marshall, Texas, courtesy of the Westmoreland family. Pieces of this flag were cut-out over the years during veterans' reunions, a common practice among the old soldiers.

Dimensions: 46" x 67"

Seventeenth Texas Infantry Regiment

Company F

This flag is a most unusual First National variant in several respects. Not as oblong as many of the type, the proportion and size, 46 x 67 inches, exclusive of the fringe, is not surprising. But the unusual star pattern, and mottos "Fearless" and "Faithfull *(sic)*" certainly are interesting.[28] The most intriguing aspect of this color is that the three bars of the field, almost always made up of three pieces of material, are instead made up of seventeen thin strips laboriously sewn together. Could this flag have been manufactured from one or more of the original prewar United States flags? The irony would be significant: "Stars and Stripes" to "Stars and Bars"!

The women of Bastrop, Texas, made this flag and presented it to Capt. E. P. Petty, commander of Company F, in July 1861. Petty was killed in 1864 at the Battle of Pleasant Hill, Louisiana.

Actions west of the Mississippi, although not warfare in as large a scale as in the Eastern or the Central Confederacy, were nevertheless equally demanding of the same leadership, courage, and sacrifice of the Confederate officer and soldier.

Captain Petty's personal journal notes, taken regularly from his enlistment up until his death in battle, have been recently republished by the University of Texas' Institute of Texan Cultures at San Antonio. Titled "Journey To Pleasant Hill," this leatherbound, two-volume set with slipcase details the daily life and endurances of a Confederate officer in one of the most inhospitable climates for warfare—southern and northwestern Louisiana.

Dimensions: 2' x 2' square

Eleventh Texas Cavalry Regiment

Guidon

This 2 x 2-foot square silk flag speaks a thousand words for the individuality of Texas Confederates.[29] The size would indicate a small unit flag, a guidon. It was preserved by a cavalryman from Company H of the Eleventh Texas Cavalry. The stars on the reverse of the canton are blue. The white canton was apparently original, although silk flags would fade very quickly. Could it have been a light blue? The flag also featured colored cords and tassels in an utter riot of color.

The Eleventh Texas Cavalry probably used this guidon early in the war while serving in the Oklahoma-Arkansas Indian Territory. Unlike many Texas cavalry regiments, it remained mounted through the war and served in most major actions of the Army of Tennessee, east of the Mississippi. The Eleventh Texas Cavalry served in approximately 150 engagements. This regiment probably used several different types of battle flags in its colorful career.

One published reference indicates that this surviving flag has nine stars encircling a larger star, with a single additional star in the left-hand corner of the canton, but it has now been confirmed that the obverse of the flag is as pictured, while the reverse (blue stars) features nine stars encircling one with an additional single star on the lower hoist corner of the canton.

The flag now rests in the care of Texas Confederate Museum, United Daughters of the Confederacy–Texas Division.

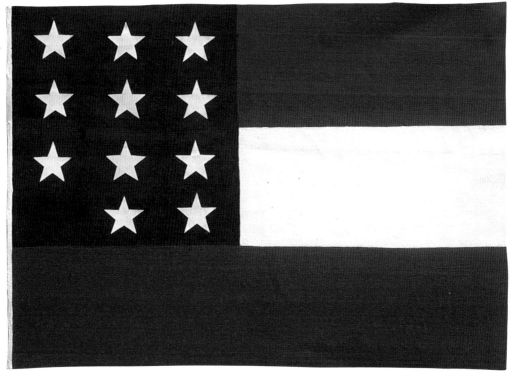

Dimensions: 5' x 7½'

Ashley Spaight's Battalion

First National Variant

Ashley Spaight's colors are of special interest here in the First National Variant pattern because *the white stars are in a noncircular pattern in the blue canton!* There is some evidence that the flag was used for the entire war.

Spaight's Battalion, officially designated the Eleventh Texas, was a combined unit of infantry and cavalry companies, technically a "legion." This Trans-Mississippi battalion was primarily assigned to the defense of the Texas and Louisiana coastline. At least one company of this unit participated in the Battle of Sabine Pass. In 1864, Spaight's Battalion was combined with Griffin's Battalion to form the Twenty-first Texas Infantry Regiment.

The illustrated flag survives today. Capt. William B. Duncan of Company F ("Moss Bluff Rebels") retained the unit colors at the end of the war. It is now cared for by the curator of the Sam Houston Regional Library and Research Center in Liberty, Texas, fifteen miles east of Houston.

The flag measures 5 x 7½ feet. Close examination of the actual flag shows no trace of a twelfth star.

Dimensions: 4½' x 8¾' approx.

First Texas Cavalry Brigade

Texas Militia

Magnolia Rangers
Stars and Bars Variant

A rather impressive variation of the "Stars and Bars," this flag was reputedly presented to the First Texas Cavalry Brigade, Texas Militia, on September 19, 1861, while the unit was encamped near Clear Creek, Galveston, Texas. The number of stars (nine) is consistent with mid-1861 First National flags.

The unit was asserted to be from nearby Cedar Bayou, Texas, and numbered sixty-four men. As the flag's reverse bar has the inscription "Instituted Jan. 17, 1861," it is possible that the flag bears the actual date of the militia unit's organization. At that time, although the secession pot was boiling over, Texas had not yet formally seceded from the Union and joined the Confederacy (February 23, 1861, and March 2, 1861, respectively).

The unit was integrated into Company K of Nichols' Ninth Texas Infantry Regiment, which dissolved after six months in March 1862 (the other Ninth Texas Infantry Regiment, Maxey's, was to see considerable action in the Central Confederacy). Many of the troops in Nichols' regiment who were mustered out joined Waul's Legion, a mixed unit of infantry and cavalry.

This silk flag measures roughly 4½ x 8¾ feet.

Certainly an impressive banner by any standards, it is a relatively recent acquisition of the Texas Confederate Museum, United Daughters of the Confederacy–Texas Division. The author is grateful for the cooperation and support of the UDC, which provided all of the information on this color.

Although faded, the flag of the Magnolia Rangers is intact and in reasonably good condition for its age. It is, however, in need of professional restoration and only requires private or corporate funding to restore it for the future.

Dimensions: 32½" x 72"

First Texas Cavalry Regiment

Company F

Ware's Tigers

Ware's Tigers was a company formed in Corpus Christi, Texas, in 1861. It carried several names and in March 1863 was designated Company F, First Texas Cavalry. In August 1862 the company fought at Corpus Christi and subsequently served along the long Texas–Louisiana coast. The unit also fought in the Battles of Pleasant Hill and Mansfield in western Louisiana in 1864.

This 32½ x 72-inch flag was probably an early battle flag of the company and could have served larger units the company may have been attached to from time to time. The red and white bars were made of silk. The thirteen stars were bordered in yellow. It is possible that the flag was originally a nine-starred flag, with the four corner stars being an 1862 addition, but it is equally possible that the maker just preferred this pattern. If that were so, the flag would probably have been made in 1862.

The maker of this flag was Mrs. Marie Terzell McLaughlin, a Louisianan by birth. Alden McLaughlin, her husband, was a corporal in the unit. This colorful relic has been restored and is in the possession of the Confederate Memorial Hall, New Orleans, Louisiana, which houses a significant collection of Confederate battle flags.

Dimensions: 34½" x 44½"

Van Dorn's Guards

Maj. Gen. Earl Van Dorn was a popular and charismatic leader whose private affairs ultimately led to his untimely assassination after the Battle of Corinth, Mississippi.

Van Dorn, while in the Virginia theater early in the war, was presented a personal twelve-starred, silk square St. Andrew's Cross battle flag, as were Generals Beauregard and Johnston, by the Cary Cousins sewing group. Soon reassigned to the Trans-Mississippi region, he took this flag with him and it was probably an inspiration for a number of St. Andrew's Cross flags with the regiments under his command.

Early in 1862 he led many of these troops, a large portion of them Texas units, across the Mississippi River in a belated attempt to reinforce Gen. Albert Sidney Johnston's Army of the Mississippi prior to the Battle of Shiloh (Pittsburg Landing) in southern Tennessee. Failing in the attempt, his troops would fight in the major engagement at Corinth, Mississippi.

One of the units that did not follow Van Dorn across the river was Daniel Shea's artillery battery. This unit called itself "Van Dorn's

Guards" – "guards" being an old title popularized by European units during the Napoleonic Wars. The illustrated flag has been attributed to this battery. The unit subsequently became part of Shea's Artillery Battalion, which later incorporated into the Eighth Texas Infantry Regiment. "Van Dorn's Guards" served its entire career in the Trans-Mississippi theater.

In the spring of 1862, Van Dorn introduced the famous Crescent Moon and Stars – the Van Dorn Pattern Flag to many if not most of the regiments in his command.

The illustrated flag features common Texas "Southern Cross" flags in that it displays an oversized star and lacks the white fimbriation (edging) between blue St. Andrew's Cross and red field. The flag also features a thinner St. Andrew's Cross than most of the type.

It is possible that this flag is "upside down." It cannot be presumed that the star was upright, as many Texas flags did not use the upright star. This flag is on display at the Museum of the Confederacy in Richmond, Virginia.

Dimensions: Varied — 30" x 40" approx.

Hardee Pattern Battle Flag

Early 1862 Issue

Battle of Shiloh
or Pittsburg Landing, Tennessee

This flag is offered as a possible flag of the Second Texas Volunteer Infantry Regiment used in the Battle of Shiloh in April 1862.

Two other Texas regiments were present on the field during this first of the major engagements outside of the Virginia theater: the Ninth Texas Infantry and the Eighth Texas Volunteer Cavalry, better known as Terry's Texas Rangers.

Four army corps had been organized by Gen. A. S. Johnston and his second-in-command, Gen. P. G. T. Beauregard. Comprising several divisions each, these corps would be commanded in the field by Major Generals Hardee, Bragg, Polk, and Breckenridge (reserve corps). The corps of Hardee, Bragg, and Polk received distinctive issue regimental battle flags. This was a different but equally effective solution to the "Stars and Bars" and "Stars and Stripes" confusion in early eastern battles.

The early issue Hardee flag is illustrated as the Second Texas Infantry Regiment was believed to be loaned to this corps for the battle,

although it was assigned to Bragg's Corps originally. It cannot be determined if the Second Texas actually carried one of these flags, but it is known that these flags were in abundance when Hardee's troops opened the surprise attack on the Federal right.

After Johnston's death in this battle, and Beauregard's transfer to coastal defense, Braxton Bragg took command of the army then known as the Army of the Mississippi. It would later gain fame as the Army of Tennessee.

As the war dragged on, many Texas regiments would join this army and fight under several different battle flags. Hardee battle flags in several variants would become the only battle flags for many of these Texas units, *but not the Second Texas Infantry*. The Second would find itself reassigned to Van Dorn's forces, which comprised mostly Trans-Mississippi troops ferried across the Mississippi River. It would fight at Corinth in late 1862 and then become part of the ill-fated Vicksburg garrison.

Dimensions: 48½" x 42½" approx.

Bragg Pattern Battle Flag

Early Issue

Battle of Shiloh
or Pittsburg Landing, Tennessee

The Bragg Pattern Battle Flag was one of the battle flags issued prior to the major action at Shiloh. The design itself was originated by Gen. P. G. T. Beauregard and ordered by him for Bragg's Corps.

The Ninth Texas Volunteer Infantry and the Second Texas Infantry were assigned to Bragg's Corps before Shiloh. It is possible but unconfirmed that these regiments could have been issued this type flag. The illustrated flag was the dominant regimental color used by Bragg's Corps at Shiloh.

The twelve stars of most Bragg battle flags were not the usual five-pointed type popularly used to designate number of states, but a very distinctive six-pointed variety. This type of star was also evident as collar rank insignia for certain general and field grade officers.

Probably the most distinctive feature of the Bragg Pattern Battle Flag is the broad pink border around the perimeter, with the exception of the hoist, which was white.

After Shiloh, the Ninth Texas Infantry was eventually assigned to Polk's Corps, combining with the Tenth and Fourteenth Texas Cavalry Regiments (Dismounted) to form what became Ector's Texas Brigade. These regiments would see action with both the Army of Tennessee and under the auspices of the Military Department of Alabama, Mississippi, and East Louisiana. Eventually, in 1863, the Thirty-second Texas Cavalry would join the brigade.

Another Texas unit was also designated as the Ninth Texas Infantry. This regiment, commanded by Colonel Nichols, served solely in the Trans-Mississippi theater, existing for only six months, and was never called to the eastern side of the Mississippi. It is usually referred to as "The Ninth Texas Infantry (Nichols')," whereas the Ninth that served in the Central Confederacy is normally referred to as "Maxey's."

Dimensions: 22" x 33"

Eighth Texas Cavalry Regiment

Bonnie Blue Variant

Terry's Texas Rangers

A few Confederate regiments from Texas achieved near legendary status, among them Terry's Texas Rangers. Confederate units of the era were commonly called by their commanding officer's surname. The Eighth Texas Volunteer Cavalry was no exception and even took the practice to exceptional heights.

This unit was one of the first to cross the Mississippi and fight in the Mississippi-Tennessee theater. Being from Texas, they were well known for their superb horsemanship (one reason why the unit remained mounted throughout the war), their keen marksmanship, and willingness to fight.

The illustrated 22 x 33-inch Bonnie Blue variant flag was possibly the first regimental color of Terry's Texas Rangers. The relatively small size of this banner may indicate a possible use as a company guidon, although with early Confederate units it is difficult, if not impossible, to standardize sizes.

The use of the Bonnie Blue by Texas regiments was not unusual but not as common as sometimes purported. The design, a central white star on a dark blue field, dates back to the independent Republic of West Florida in 1810. The star on the Terry's Texas Rangers' flag is very striking, perhaps more so due to its inverted or tilted placement. Inverted stars may have merely been the individual preference of the flag's maker. One theory has it that the inverted or tilted star stood for people in rebellion.[30]

Another such theory (or rumor) was that, regardless of the type flag (Bonnie Blue, State Lone Star, and others), the practice of tilting the star may have come from the Army of the Republic of Texas. It was said that when in combat (usually border skirmishes with Mexican troops), the troops would fly the Lone Star Flag (the third flag of the Republic of Texas) upside down so that the red bar on the field would be on top.[31] This might have been done to avoid the possibility of the correct white top bar being mistaken for a surrender flag or a sign of no quarter. As Texas had been a republic sixteen years prior to secession, aged veterans or their wives may have continued the tradition.

The third theory is that some of the flags, made by women who belonged to the Masonic Eastern Star organization, used their inverted star symbol. Interestingly, at the St. Mary's Catholic Church in Victoria, Texas, a stained glass window is adorned with an Eastern Star over two Confederate-type flags. It was placed there as a Confederate memorial around 1900.

Regardless of theories, it is probable that there were no official guidelines of placing the star upright in any Texas flag.

In addition to the inverted star, the lettering "Terry's Texas Ranger's" is interesting, as the apostrophe in the word "Ranger's" is not grammatically correct.

The illustrated flag survives today in the care of the Decorative and Industrial Arts Collection of the Chicago Historical Society. This cooperative organization provided a photograph of the flag, from which the illustration in this book was rendered.

Perhaps one day our "Yankee" friends can be convinced to return it to Texas.

U.S. Population (1860 Census)*

"NORTHERN" STATES AND TERRITORIES

State	Population	State	Population
Maine	619,958	Minnesota	172,793
New Hampshire	372,072	Oregon	52,506
Vermont	315,827	California	384,770
Massachusetts	1,231,494	Kansas	143,645
Rhode Island	174,621	Delaware	110,655
Connecticut	460,670	Maryland	644,777
New York	3,851,561	Missouri	1,086,244
New Jersey	676,084	Kentucky	920,077
Pennsylvania	2,916,018	Nebraska	28,893
Ohio	2,277,919	Dakota	4,839
Indiana	1,350,802	Washington	11,624
Michigan	754,291	Utah	50,009
Illinois	1,691,238	New Mexico	92,023
Wisconsin	768,485	Dist. of Columbia	72,140
Iowa	682,002		
		Total	21,872,995

"SOUTHERN" STATES

State	Population	State	Population
Virginia	1,102,312	Alabama	520,785
North Carolina	677,261	Mississippi	450,462
South Carolina	312,830	Louisiana	334,911
Georgia	620,527	Texas	420,567
Florida	92,741	Arkansas	329,671
Tennessee	870,856		
		Total	5,782,923

* Slaves not included

SLAVE POPULATION (1860)

State	Population	State	Population
Alabama	435,132	Mississippi	436,696
Arkansas	111,104	Missouri	114,965
Delaware	1,798	North Carolina	331,081
Florida	61,753	South Carolina	402,541
Georgia	462,230	Tennessee	275,784
Kentucky	225,490	Texas	180,388
Louisiana	332,520	Virginia	490,887
Maryland	87,188	District of Columbia	3,181
		Total	3,952,738

Dimensions: unknown — 30" x 40" approx.

Van Dorn Pattern Battle Flag

Crescent Moon and Thirteen Stars

Gen. Earl Van Dorn introduced his own pattern flag in early 1862 — the famous Crescent Moon and Thirteen Stars — to many units under his command, including Texas units. Perhaps he wanted to more clearly distinguish his corps, which was to join Gen. A. S. Johnston's army as it advanced to Shiloh.

The Van Dorn flags were not the only Confederate forces to fly the Crescent Moon emblem. Early South Carolina secession banners used this device. It was often seen in the Missouri theater of operations as well.

It is possible that Texas regiments carried the above type flags while under Van Dorn's command. However, some variants of the St. Andrew's Cross type have also been associated with Van Dorn. Therefore, it becomes difficult to state with absolute certainty when and if the Crescent Moon and Thirteen Stars flags were actually used by Texas units. While in Alabama, circa 1864, the above-mentioned Texas regiments were issued a new type of twelve-starred St. Andrew's Cross flag (Cameron manufacture),

which was commonly associated with Gen. N. B. Forrest's cavalry corps and Polk's/Stuart's corps of 1864.

The illustrated flag is based on the remnants of the battle flag of the Ninth Texas Cavalry. Descendants of a cavalryman of that unit still possess the flag. According to family tradition, this flag was used by the Ninth Texas at Elk Horn (Pea Ridge). After the battle Van Dorn reputedly copied the flag and made it the standard pattern for his troops. It is true that the Crescent Moon was a commonly used symbol in Missouri. The Ninth Texas served at Oak Hill (Wilson's Creek), Missouri, prior to Elk Horn.

A major difference between the Ninth's flag and other Van Dorn Pattern Flags is the shade of red. The illustrated flag utilizes the shade of red seen on most Van Dorn Pattern Flags. The Ninth Texas' flag is darker, almost maroon.

Texas regiments that could have used this flag in 1862 and 1863 were the Third, Sixth, Ninth, Tenth, Eleventh, Fourteenth, and Twenty-seventh cavalry regiments.

Dimensions: 36" x 40" approx.

Twelfth Texas Volunteer Cavalry

Partisan Rangers

Hill's Plantation, Arkansas

This swallowtail battle flag represents one of the many contradictions found when one attempts to logically follow Texas Confederate flag use.

The illustrated flag was allegedly captured at Hill's Plantation, Arkansas, from the Twelfth Texas Cavalry on July 7, 1862.[32] The flag is also associated with a unit called the "Partisan Rangers." The Twelfth Texas Cavalry Regiment was previously issued a "Beauregard" St. Andrew's Cross type battle flag in December 1861. It is believed that the Twelfth was engaged in a skirmish at that time.

"Partisan Rangers" was a name associated with several other regiments, while the Twelfth Texas Cavalry Regiment has become associated today with the label "Parson's Texas Cavalry." The troops in Parson's regiment were known as "Parson's Dragoons" early in the war.

It is possible that this was a company flag and perhaps the name "Partisan Rangers" is a company affiliation. Its 36 x 40-inch size suggests that it could have been used either as a regimental flag or a company guidon.[33]

The flag was made of wool or a wool mix, and the white star of cotton. The blue numeral on the silk star appeared only on the obverse side, although the stitching could be seen on the reverse.

Dimensions: 4' x 4' square

Ninth Texas Cavalry

Corinth

Although there is strong evidence that early in 1862 the Ninth Texas Cavalry carried the Crescent Moon and Thirteen Stars Van Dorn Pattern Flag, there is also evidence that the regiment, serving as dismounted cavalry at the Battle of Corinth, lost a silk St. Andrew's Cross battle flag to Union combat forces in hand-to-hand fighting. This would date the flag's use in October of 1862, the time period when silk St. Andrew's Cross battle flags were fading out of favor to more durable fabrics.

The existence of this flag wreaks havoc with the perhaps wishful theory that all Van Dorn units, when Major General Van Dorn introduced his own pattern flag in early 1862, used only that flag. It is possible that this silk battle flag was a replacement for the Ninth's surviving (but extremely tattered) Van Dorn Battle Flag, but that is yet to be substantiated.

While Van Dorn did introduce his own distinctive pattern flag to his command, it is known that he personally used a silk St. Andrew's

Cross battle flag through Corinth. Earlier in the war Van Dorn, as one of the three leading general officers in Virginia, had been presented a prototype silk battle flag (as had Generals Beauregard and Johnston) by Constance Cary and her two cousins, Hetty and Jennie. These women were destined to produce many of the early silk battle flags of the various state units which would eventually become the Army of Northern Virginia.

These early flags were similar to the silk battle flags made by the Wigfall ladies for the Fourth and Fifth Texas infantry regiments, with a light red field and yellow border, although the hoist was usually dark blue. The illustrated flag measures a similar 4 x 4 feet square.[34]

It is hoped that more evidence of Van Dorn flags used by Texas regiments will be obtained, perhaps by the surfacing of additional flags from private collections or from soldiers' letters and diaries not yet discovered or considered in the context of battle flags.

Dimensions: unknown 4' x 6' est.

Sixth Texas Infantry Regiment

Trans-Mississippi Theater

Arkansas Post (Fort Hindman)

This flag (the illustration based on three independent descriptions) was handmade in 1862 by Mrs. Richard Owens, a mercantile store owner in Victoria, Texas. The flag was forwarded to the regiment after it had completed its training at Camp McCullough in Victoria. It was captured, along with the regiment, at Arkansas Post, Arkansas, in January 1863.

Although the flag remained in the North, the regiment was exchanged and returned to the South for further service in May 1863. Exhibited in Chicago, Illinois, in 1863, the regimental color was described by the *Chicago Tribune* as the "most showy" of the captured Confederate flags.[35] It was made of merino and satin with a white fringe.

Presumably the flag was destroyed in the great Chicago fire of 1871. The pattern for this flag survived the war and may still exist in a private collection. The measurements of this regimental color are unknown, but it was noted to be larger than an ordinary regimental flag, probably about 4 x 6 feet. Some Hispanic troops from the San Antonio area served in this regiment.

The Sixth Texas, along with other Texas and Arkansas units, joined Cleburne's Division, Hardee's Corps, Army of Tennessee, in mid-1863. They were issued dark blue Hardee flags, probably bordered in white.

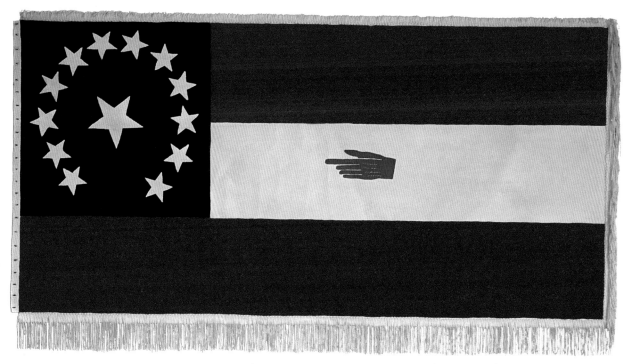

Dimensions: 3' x 6' approx.

Unknown Regiment

First National Variant

Arkansas Post (Fort Hindman)

Several Texas regiments were captured by Union forces at Arkansas Post with the surrender of the Texas and Arkansas troops garrisoned there in January of 1863. Seven Confederate colors were taken with the garrison.[36] The illustrated flag has been ascribed as belonging to either the Sixth Texas Infantry or the Twelfth Texas Cavalry Regiment.[37] The Twelfth Texas, however, did not serve at Arkansas Post and the Sixth Texas had a flag of its own. It is possible, however, that the Sixth had both a First National Pattern Flag and the "Shield" flag already noted. It is also possible that this was a company flag of any one of the regiments serving there at the time (dismounted Texas cavalry regiments being the Fifteenth, Seventeenth, Eighteenth, Twenty-fourth, and Twenty-fifth, along with the Sixth

and Tenth Texas infantry regiments). One Union battle report stated that the colors of the Tenth Texas Infantry Regiment were captured.[38]

Restorers of the illustrated flag found the probable maker's name "Kate Phillips" under the blue glove.[39] Perhaps one day her name will be associated with one of the regiments and the unit identity of this flag will be solved.

It was not an unusual oblong shape (for National Flag types) and measured 3 x 6 feet. A large white fringe enhanced the flag. The flag was made of cotton with silk stars. Note the unusual horseshoe shape of the star pattern, possibly indicating a cavalry unit.

This original flag is on display at the Colonel Harold B. Simpson Confederate Research Center, Hill College, Hillsboro, Texas.

Dimensions: 37½" x 69"

Wilson Guards

First National Variant

Arkansas Post (Fort Hindman)

At least two of the seven Confederate colors captured at Arkansas Post have apparently survived. This example, "Wilson Guards," probably originated as a company flag. The red identification, pink silk border, star, and ties dressed up an otherwise ordinary example of a First National type flag. Note the white bar is wider than the two red bars on the field.

The flag measures 37½ x 69 inches and survives today in a private collection.[40]

There is some support to the possibility that this may be the color of the Tenth Texas Infantry. Federal sources indicated that a flag of the Tenth Texas was captured. The Wilson Guards is probably a reference to a company from Wilson County, Texas. The pinkish star confirms Texas origins.

There is tenuous evidence that companies from the Wilson County area eventually served with the Tenth Texas Infantry. The eleven stars indicate 1861 manufacture.

Dimensions: 41" x 52"

Lone Star Flag

Port Hudson

Located approximately twenty miles north of Baton Rouge, Louisiana, on the Mississippi River, the sleepy town of Port Hudson once served as the southern bastion protecting Confederate cross-river traffic while Vicksburg served the same purpose to the north. Both were targeted by Federal forces in the spring of 1863. Gen. Nathaniel Banks, with Union forces from the captured port of New Orleans, attacked Port Hudson on March 15, 1863, but was repulsed. The campaign against the town continued, however, and the Confederate forces there surrendered on July 9, 1863, five days after Vicksburg fell.

The Mississippi was effectively closed to commercial and military traffic and the western Confederacy was cut off from the east. At least two Texas units served near Port Hudson during this period: Burnet's First Battalion of Volunteer Sharpshooters and the Seventh Texas Volunteer Infantry Regiment.

The illustrated Lone Star Flag was allegedly captured by Federal troops possibly during their unsuccessful attack on March 15.[41] It is more probable that this flag belonged to Burnet's unit because the Seventh Texas Infantry had been exchanged from the Fort Donelson surrender.

The star on this cotton flag is tilted in the opposite direction of the First Texas' flag used at Sharpsburg (Antietam). Of note is the substantially wider red lower bar on the field. This flag measured approximately 41 x 52 inches. Aside from the use of Hood's Texas Brigade, no other large Texas State Flags have been confirmed to be used by Texas Confederate regiments.[42]

Burnet's Sharpshooters were perhaps the only Texas unit to return to the state after the closure of the Mississippi. In December 1863 they reputedly went back across the river in small boats, a difficult but not impossible task.

The Seventh Texas Infantry, under Granbury, joined the Army of Tennessee, becoming part of Granbury's Texas Brigade.

Thirty-second Texas Cavalry Regiment

Bonnie Blue Flag

The accompanying illustration is a generic depiction of a pattern of flag called the "Bonnie Blue Flag." The single white star on a blue field had its origins in Florida in 1810. It is possible that the First and Second National flags of the Republic of Texas were Bonnie Blue variants in design and origin. If this is true, it can be argued that the Texas Lone Star Flag, emblazoned with a red and white field, is also a variant. However, it was the Bonnie Blue's use by the seceding state of Mississippi in January 1861 that inspired the song which gave the design its name and immortality. The Bonnie Blue Flag was not the only secession flag, but it is certainly the most remembered.

The shade of blue in the flag probably varied with the availability of materials, and there seemed to be no rule that the star had to be placed upright. Tilted stars were commonplace.

There were two regiments called the Thirty-second Texas Cavalry. One served in the Trans-Mississippi, while the other served in the East with the Army of Tennessee. The Trans-Mississippi Thirty-second Texas Cavalry, also called the Thirty-sixth Texas Cavalry, was formed in 1862 near Fredericksburg, Texas, from troops whose initial one-year enlistments had expired. Many men from the First Texas Cavalry joined this unit, including one F. G. Crawford, who noted in his memoirs that Mrs. Sam (Mary) Maverick and other women from San Antonio made and presented to the regiment a large Bonnie Blue Flag made of silk. According to Crawford, their Bonnie Blue was never captured.[43]

It is hoped by the author that the illustrated flag still exists or at least has been documented in photographs. An 1893 reunion photograph shows what may be the flag being held by one of the veterans.[44] Unfortunately, this dark flag (if it is a flag) is limp on the flagpole and cannot be fully seen. The Library of the Daughters of the Republic of Texas at the Alamo in San Antonio, Texas, has a reference to a Confederate Bonnie

Blue Flag with gold fringe. This reference is possibly to the Thirty-second's flag or the flag of another unit.

Another possible Confederate Bonnie Blue type is the flag of the Alamo City Guards, a unit from San Antonio. A photograph of this flag exists at the above-referenced library. On the flag is the Latin phrase "FIAT JUSTITIA RUAT COELUM" over the single star. "ALAMO CITY GUARDS" is stylishly placed under the star. It is unknown if this is a genuine Civil War-era flag or a later reunion flag.

A flag at Texas A&M University is identified with Ross' Cavalry Brigade. It is a Bonnie Blue variant, very ornate with a gold star and ornamentation. This flag is definitely not a wartime banner. It is believed to be a postwar reunion flag used for parades and the like.[45] Actual Confederate heraldry was discouraged in the Reconstruction-era South for many years.

White Males Technically Available for Military Service (18–45 years) in Each State

FREE STATES

New York	778,000	California	76,000
Pennsylvania	581,000	Connecticut	92,000
Ohio	468,000	Iowa	135,000
Illinois	342,000	Kansas	21,000
Indiana	270,000	Minnesota	32,000
Massachusetts	246,000	New Hampshire	65,000
Michigan	150,000	Rhode Island	35,000
Maine	125,000	Vermont	63,000
Wisconsin	155,000	Oregon	10,000
New Jersey	134,000		
		Total	3,778,000

BORDER STATES

Delaware	22,000	Kentucky	186,000
Maryland	120,000	Missouri	211,000
		Total	539,000

REBEL STATES

Virginia	221,000	Arkansas	65,000
North Carolina	132,000	Florida	16,000
Tennessee	167,000	Mississippi	71,000
Georgia	119,000	South Carolina	60,000
Alabama	106,000	Texas	84,000
Louisiana	75,000		
		Total	1,116,000

RECAPITULATION

Free States	3,778,000	Rebel States	1,116,000
Border States	539,000		
	4,317,000		

Dimensions: 21" x 36"

Thirty-second Texas Cavalry Regiment

Swallowtail First National Variant

Trans-Mississippi

This primarily wool flag was probably not the regimental flag of the Trans-Mississippi Thirty-second Texas Cavalry but possibly was a cavalry guidon. The size of 21 x 36 inches is not conclusive as to type of use, but the numeral in the single star would suggest the possibility of regimental level use.

The swallowtail on this flag seems to be crudely cut, so it is possible that this flag originally had a standard fly edge and was converted to a swallowtail. On the surviving flag are what appear to be bloodstains on the white bar near the swallowtail. It is possible that the swallowtail was created from a battle-damaged edge.

This interesting color is in a private collection in Texas and is well cared for and in reasonably good condition. Information provided with a photograph of the flag indicated that it was linked to Col. Peter Wood's Thirty-second Texas Cavalry Regiment (a.k.a. Thirty-sixth) which

called themselves the "Racoon Roughs." A Bonnie Blue Flag was probably the regimental flag, as F. G. Crawford was in Company B of this regiment.

Another regiment also called the Thirty-second Texas Cavalry served primarily dismounted east of the Mississippi with the Army of Tennessee and like the Thirty-second Texas of the Trans-Mississippi had an eventful career. It was often erroneously referred to as the Fifteenth Cavalry, which can create confusion as another Texas regiment called the Fifteenth Texas Cavalry (Dismounted) also served in the Army of Tennessee combined with the Sixth Texas Infantry in Granbury's Texas Brigade. The Thirty-second Texas Cavalry, although it also briefly served in Granbury's Brigade, apparently saw most of its service with Ector's Texas Brigade in the same army.

Dimensions: unknown

Maury's Division

Missouri Type Battle Flag

Second Texas Infantry Regiment
Waul's Legion
Vicksburg

A common flag of Confederate regiments at Vicksburg was the "Missouri Type" battle flag. At least two variants of this type of flag exist, the illustrated type color and the same design except with a blue field and red border without stars. The depicted flag is the personal flag of Maj. Gen. Dabney Maury, a divisional commander during the winter of 1862–63 campaign. Maury was a Virginian, so it was very likely he adopted a flag prevalent in his command. At least one other division, J. S. Bowen's, used this flag in quantity. During the siege, General Forney commanded Maury's Division.

The Second Texas Infantry and Waul's Texas Legion (infantry contingent) served together in Maury's Division. They saw significant action during the first and second Vicksburg actions. One part of the Vicksburg defenses was called the "Second Texas Lunette." Waul's infantry helped repulse a major Federal attack and captured a Federal stand of colors. It is unknown what flags the two units flew in the first seven months of 1863.

Hardee, Bragg, Van Dorn, and the above type battle flags are all possibles. There is an unconfirmed reference to the Second Texas surrendering a First National Flag at Vicksburg, but this may have been a larger garrison-type flag that possibly flew over the Lunette.

This commentary is at best speculation but suggests the possibilities that might stimulate research and a re-reading of letters, documents, and reminiscences of veterans. The finding of one or two of the flags of the Second Texas and Waul's Legion of this period would add a piece to the puzzle.

After surrender, parole, and reorganization, the Second Texas and the infantry of Waul's Legion carried the Second National Flag as part of the Galveston defenses.

Dimensions: 4' x 8'

Twentieth Texas Infantry Regiment

First National Pattern

Without argument the most ornate of the known Confederate battle flags, the regimental colors of the Twentieth Texas Infantry had one distinctive feature that might be easily overlooked by the novice or amateur historian: Unlike the overwhelming majority of Texas-produced First National type battle flags, *this banner lacks the larger central star within the circle of stars in the canton.*

The thirteen stars would indicate an 1862 to mid-1863 manufacture. As this unit primarily served in coastal defense, the large 4 x 8-foot flag would not be considered unwieldy or unusual.[46] The illustration cannot adequately convey the grandeur of this magnificent color in its prime.

A flag with this much gold color would be surprising only if it were not made of expensive silk—which, of course, it was!

This magnificent flag rests in the collection of the Texas Confederate Museum, United Daughters of the Confederacy–Texas Division.

Dimensions: 4' x 6'

Thirty-third Texas Cavalry Regiment

Second National Battle Flag

After the Provisional Congress of the Confederate States of America evolved into the first Congress of the new nation, talk surfaced about adopting a new National Flag. The decision was delayed until 1863. By then, the realities of war had turned Southern hearts grim with resolve to rid themselves of all vestiges of the old Union. At the eleventh hour of the congressional session, a new design was passed through Congress. The design incorporated a version of the square Army of Northern Virginia's battle flag designs and added a white field to emblazon the battle flag canton.

Although communications with the Trans-Mississippi region were becoming increasingly difficult due to the Union campaign closing in on Vicksburg, word of the change of flags surely got through, although the implementation was probably slow. All comments about the military use of the First National Flag apply to this flag. Army headquarters throughout the South, even of generals in the Army of Northern Virginia,

flew this flag. The flags of Brig. Gen. Jubal Early and Maj. Gen. J. E. B. Stuart survive today. This flag was used by the Confederacy until April 1865, when a red vertical stripe was added to the fly edge (the Third National Pattern). It is doubtful if the Third type saw service anywhere but near Richmond, Virginia.

Even with the advent of various distinctive "issue" battle flag types by the time of adoption of the Second National Flag, it was sometimes issued as a battle flag to regiments, including the Thirty-third Texas Cavalry. This regiment was formed in April 1863 utilizing the Fourteenth Texas Cavalry Battalion as its nucleus. It served primarily in South Texas along the Rio Grande River. One of its officers who eventually rose to the rank of colonel, Santos Benevides, was the highest ranking Hispanic to attain the field command in Confederate service. It should be recognized that 10,000 Hispanics, mostly from Texas, served in the conflict. Seventy-five percent fought for the South while the remainder maintained allegiance to the Union. An Hispanic lieutenant of the Sixth Texas, surnamed Rios, was killed at Chickamauga.

This cotton flag was probably issued to the regiment shortly after the adoption of the new National Flag. It measures 4 x 6 feet and survives today in a private collection.[47]

The larger central star suggests that it was probably made in Texas. Other Second National Flags were issued to Texas regiments, especially those that were re-equipped or were organized in mid-to-late 1863. Most featured white edging on the blue St. Andrew's Cross.

The first official use of the Second National Flag was to cover the coffin of Lt. Gen. Thomas J. "Stonewall" Jackson as he lay in state at Richmond. This sparked the title "The Jackson Flag." Another name by which this type flag was known was "The Stainless Banner."

Although the service of Hispanics and Native Americans with the Confederacy, especially with or in association with Texas Confederates, is well documented, there is evidence that some Southern African-Americans, both slaves and Freedmen, served the Confederate military usually in a support capacity. However, one purported militia unit, the Mobile Guards, supposedly made up of African-American Freedmen, may have seen combat in the waning days of the war. Of course, the primary African-American military contribution in the Civil War was with the Union. The first engagement between African-American Union soldiers and Confederates was at Honey Springs, Indian Territory, in 1863. The Confederates happened to be Texans. Also in that battle, Native Americans fought on both sides.

Dimensions: 52" x 84"

Waul's Texas Legion
And/Or Second Texas Infantry Regiment

Second National Variant

Technically, a legion consisted of mixed infantry and cavalry. Waul's Texas Legion comprised twelve infantry companies and six cavalry companies. The twelve infantry companies had sufficient manpower to justify status as a regiment.

Waul's infantry component served at Vicksburg. Captured on July 4, 1863, with the rest of the surrendered garrison, these companies were paroled rather than exchanged west of the Mississippi. As soon as its parole expired, the infantry was returned and took up arms again, this time as part of the Galveston coastal defenses. The brigade they were attached to also contained the Second Texas Infantry Regiment, itself a Vicksburg veteran.

The illustrated flag may have been issued to Waul's Legion, the Second Texas Infantry

Regiment, or identical type flags may have been given to both and other units in the brigade. The honor was painted in gold on a strip of cloth sewn to the field. This flag was a true battle flag; i.e., a regimental. It measured 52 x 84 inches. The canton itself measured an almost square 34 x 32 inches.[48]

The cavalry companies in Waul's Texas Legion were stranded east of the Mississippi with the fall of Vicksburg. They were attached to Lt. Gen. Nathan Bedford Forrest's Cavalry and served under his command. As such, the unit may have fought under several possible battle flags.

This flag rests in the care of the Texas Confederate Museum, United Daughters of the Confederacy–Texas Division.

Dimensions: 4' x 6'

Seventeenth Texas Cavalry (Dismounted)

Second National Variant

Trans-Mississippi Department

Not all the companies of the Seventeenth Texas Cavalry Regiment (Dismounted) were captured at Arkansas Post in January 1863. Those elements of the regiment not captured continued to serve west of the Mississippi River. This Second National variant was used by these troops and features interesting departures from what would normally be seen in a Second National type.

The gold-painted stars, overlapping fimbriation on the blue cross in the canton, white fringe, and red edging on the field make this color both interesting and unique.[49] The illustrated flag measured approximately 4 x 6 feet. It presently rests in the care of the Smith County Historical Society, Tyler, Texas.

Dimensions: 34½" x 32"

Unknown Texas Regiment

Second National Variant

Discovered in 1994 near Nacogdoches, Texas, this short, 34½ x 32-inch silk flag was considered by this examiner to be a square variation of what normally should have been a rectangular flag. However, flag historian Howard Michael Madaus is of the opinion that the length of this flag was probably 4½ x 5½ feet. It is not that uncommon for silk flags to deteriorate even in storage. Certainly, as a square flag it would be a dramatic exception. However, it has been said that some units that used the Second National Flag as a battle flag would cut off the white field.

There are other features that are clearly unusual about this color. While the blue silk cross is fairly typical with appliqué stars, the red field of the canton is not a field at all but four triangles of red silk sewn onto the white main field. The white fimbriation is actually the gap between the red and blue silk appliqué. This rugged construction is noteworthy.

Second National Flags were never seen in the same abundance as the Stars and Bars (First National Flags) because of the variety of flags already available to individual units.

Dimensions: 34" x 66"

Border's Regiment

Texas Volunteer Cavalry

This flag has been asserted to be the colors of John P. Border's Regiment of Volunteer Cavalry. However, Border's "regiment" was not formed until his battalion and Fulcrod's Battalion of Cadets (Texas Volunteer Cavalry) combined after the date of the adoption of the Second National Flag of the Confederacy (May 1863). Because of this fact, it is assumed that Border's Battalion first used this flag before the organization of the regiment.

That may indeed be the case. However, with communications and manufacturing limitations as they were, it is not inconceivable that the flag could have been made in 1863 and used for the first time by Border's Regiment, even with the adoption of the new Second National Flag. The flag was a regimental color, and units west of the Mississippi had extreme latitude in the selection of their flags.

The flag measures 34 x 66 inches. The stars are cotton while the remainder of the flag is "bunting," except for the white canvas pieces reinforcing the eyelets. The white bar is wider than the two red bars on the field.[50]

Dimensions: 24" x 36"

Unknown Unit

Second National Variant

Chickamauga

A Second National battle color, this flag is on display at the Terrell Heritage Museum, Terrell, Texas. The caption under its display case reads: *"Chickamauga Battle Flag–1863."* The flag was received by the museum from the descendants of Capt. Sidney J. Bass, a Mississippian who served in the Army of Tennessee.

The flag situation in Bragg's Army of Tennessee in late 1863 was probably at the height of chaos. Hardee, Polk, ANV, and Bragg patterns were present, as well as Bonnie Blues, National Flags, and Van Dorn patterns.

In the spring of 1864, in a deliberate attempt to rectify the battlefield confusion of so many different flags, newly appointed commander Gen. Joe Johnston issued orders to retire all old battle flags in favor of his rectangular, thirteen-star St. Andrew's Cross battle flag (the same flag incorrectly accepted today as *the* battle flag of the Confederacy).

Brigadier General Cleburne's Division, by official exception, retained their Hardee flags. Other regiments had received new twelve-star St. Andrew's Cross battle flags which were similar to Johnston's flag and therefore were retained.

Additionally, Second Nationals were used in combat by some regiments during the Atlanta Campaign, as well as square ANV style flags brought up by troops as coastal garrison reinforcements near Atlanta. Almost all of these flags featured a blue St. Andrew's Cross on a red field.

The illustrated flag cannot be confirmed as a Texas regimental color. However, the large, central, Texas-style star helps to encourage the possibility. The lack of white fimbriation along the edges of the cross makes the Texas argument stronger, although research shows that this style was not uncommon across the different theaters. National flags were often used as temporary battle flags while a regiment was awaiting issuance of a "pattern" flag.

The small size of this flag is not conclusive as to whether this was a company flag or a regimental standard. Army of Tennessee flags have a tendency for smaller proportions than do ANV flags.

Artillery – Galveston Defenses

Second National (Mid-1863 to 1865)

Flags used by artillery units in defense of the Confederate Texas coast merit the honor of being battle flags. Although the port of Galveston was seized early in the war, it was retaken by Texan troops in dramatic fashion on January 1, 1863, and became one of the chief ports open to blockade runners.

Artillery units that protected coastal installations used large flags, normally one of the two National types. This 5½ x 12-foot flag has been identified with Maj. Charles R. Benton, chief of ordnance (artillery), Galveston defenses. More closely conforming in length with the Second National pattern adopted by the Confederate

Congress in May 1863 and the naval ensign adopted thereafter, this flag and others like it could have flown over the Galveston defenses from the summer of 1863 to the end of the war. Flags issued to infantry, cavalry, and field artillery were normally shorter on the fly end.

This flag is noted to be made of bunting, probably a wool-cotton mix. The rectangular canton is noteworthy. It is in the collection of the Louisiana Historical Association, Confederate Memorial Hall, New Orleans, Louisiana. (All information noted concerning this flag has been provided by the Confederate Memorial Hall.)

Dimensions: 28" x 52" approx.

Ector's Texas Brigade

Polk Pattern Battle Flag

Ector's Texas Brigade, comprising at least Maxey's Ninth Texas Infantry Regiment and the Tenth, Fourteenth, and eventually the Thirty-second Texas Cavalry Regiments (Dismounted), was organized in early 1863. By the winter of that year it would be found assigned to Polk's Corps. The regiments in this brigade possibly received late issue Polk battle flags in the latter part of that year. It is possible that at least the Ninth Texas flew this flag at Murfreesboro (Stone's River) as part of Vaughn's Brigade in December 1862–January 1863.

The flag was originated by Lt. Gen. Leonidas Polk for the regiments in his corps prior to Shiloh. It was one of the three most common flags at that action, along with the Hardee and Bragg types. At that time the red cross may not had a white fimbriation (edging); however, the white edge appeared as the design matured (as reflected in this illustration). Polk was an Episcopalian bishop prior to the war. His St. George's Cross style flags may have been inspired by that religious service.

The illustrated type flag was retired after two years, in the winter of 1863–64. At that time Polk's command, which included Ector's Texas Brigade, was part of the Department of Alabama, Mississippi and East Louisiana. A new type of battle flag was issued there to Polk's units. Provided by the Military Department of Alabama, Mississippi, and East Louisiana, they were of Cameron manufacture, featuring twelve stars in a St. Andrew's Cross. This type flag is illustrated as the flag of the Third Texas Cavalry, Ross' Cavalry Brigade. It is highly probable that Ector's Brigade was issued Cameron flags.

Perhaps worn out from the brigade's very active service fighting with the Army of Tennessee in Atlanta, and then again in Alabama, the Cameron types were possibly retired in favor of the square ANV type. In March 1865, Ector's Brigade would surrender their last flags.

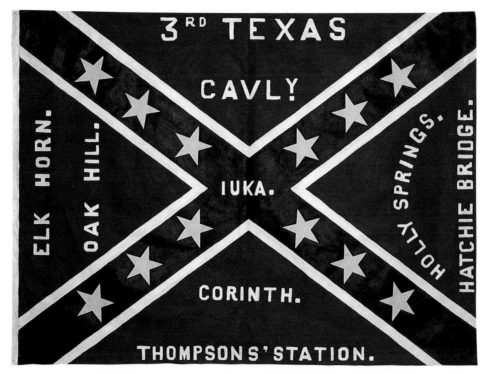

Dimensions: 42½" x 52"

Third Texas Cavalry Regiment

Ross' Cavalry Brigade

In early 1864, the regiments of Forrest's Cavalry Corps and Polk's Command were wintering in the jurisdiction of the Military Department of Alabama, Mississippi, and East Louisiana. They were issued twelve-starred cotton flags produced in some quantity by James Cameron of Mobile, Alabama. When Gen. Joe Johnston, newly in command of the Army of Tennessee, saw these new flags in the possession of Polk's Corps (later Stuart's, when Polk would fall to a single, well-aimed, Union cannon shot), Johnston was reputedly inspired to procure a similar flag for the entire army, but with thirteen smaller stars.

The flags of the Third, Ninth, and Twenty-seventh Texas Cavalry survived the war. The whereabouts of the Twenty-seventh's colors is unknown. The flag of the Ninth Texas Cavalry is in a private collection, but the flag of the Third Cavalry rests at the Texas State Archives in reasonably good condition after having been cased and restored. It is one of the few flags to be profesionally preserved in the Texas Archives' storage facility. This flag measures approximately 42½ x 52 inches. The hoist edge is missing on the surviving material, but a photograph of the flag of the Twenty-seventh Texas Cavalry (showing a twelve-starred flag but often misidentified as a "Johnston battle flag"), although badly tattered, indicates a white hoist edge.

It is now very probable that Ector's Texas Brigade, comprising at least the Ninth Texas Infantry, Fourteenth Texas Cavalry (Dismounted), and the Tenth Texas Cavalry (Dismounted) would also have received this type flag because they were in French's Division in Alabama at the time of this new issue flag. By the time of the Atlanta battles the brigade was in the thick of the fight in the summer of 1864. By 1865, the brigade was flying square Army of Northern Virginia-type flags in the defense of Spanish Fort, near Mobile, Alabama.

The illustrated Department of Alabama flag of these regiments differed from the official Johnston Army of Tennessee flags in these respects: twelve stars instead of thirteen, larger stars, white battle honors sewn on the field and some dimensional variance. The Johnston's flag battle honors were apparently stenciled on the white fimbriation of the cross in black or dark blue.

It should be noted that at least a third, if not more, of units in the Army of Tennessee carried this twelve-star battle flag. This and the blue Hardee (Cleburne variant) flag were the flags of most Texans in the Army of Tennessee in 1864. Only one Texas unit, Good's-Douglas Battery, would possibly use the Johnston flag in this period.

Capt. Samuel Richardson, Third Texas Cavalry Regiment.
— Photo courtesy The Museum of the Confederacy, Richmond, Virginia

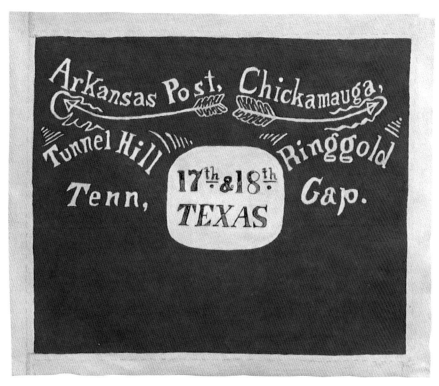

Dimensions: 31" x 38"

Seventeenth and Eighteenth Texas Cavalry Regiment (Dismounted)

Cleburne's Division, Army of Tennessee

Previously noted was the surrender of Fort Hindman/Arkansas Post in January 1863. Two Texas infantry and five Texas cavalry regiments were captured at this Trans-Mississippi post. The two infantry units were the Sixth and Tenth Texas; the cavalry units were the Seventeenth, Eighteenth, Twenty-fourth, and Twenty-fifth Texas. All were exchanged by the summer of 1863 and immediately assigned to the Army of Tennessee east of the Mississippi, the area they were most needed. Having been embarrassed somewhat by the circumstances of surrender (there was some question as to whether the surrender had been a bit premature, although battle had been joined), the Texas troops cleared themselves of any doubts with valorious service in Granbury's Texas Brigade of Maj. Gen. Patrick Cleburne's Division, Army of Tennessee.

When exchanged, all the regiments were understrength. They were reorganized into "combined regiments." The Sixth and Fifteenth Infantry was formed from these two regiments with the Tenth Texas Infantry and Thirty-second Dismounted Cavalry (both of which would be reassigned later, the Tenth Texas to full regimental status and the Thirty-second to Ector's Brigade). The Seventeenth, Eighteenth, Twenty-fourth, and Twenty-fifth Cavalry (Dismounted) then formed the Seventeenth and Eighteenth Cavalry Regiment (Dismounted).

Also joining Granbury's Brigade was the Seventh Texas Infantry Regiment, which had crossed the Mississippi voluntarily sometime before. Granbury himself would command the brigade only to fall, along with General Cleburne, leading it in action during Hood's ill-fated attack at Franklin, Tennessee, in late 1864.

The newly reformed regiments, without equipment or flags, would most certainly have been issued new dark blue Hardee Pattern colors. These featured central white discs of oval or somewhat circular design. By this time Hardee flags also featured wide white borders. They would have seen much subsequent action, such as the major battles at Chickamauga, Missionary Ridge (Tunnel Hill), and Ringgold Gap.

In early 1864, however, Gen. Joe Johnston ordered that at least all "old style" battle flags, which included the Bragg, Polk, and Hardee types, were to be retired in favor of a new issue battle flag, a rectangular, thirteen-star St. Andrew's Cross type which was to gain great favor throughout the postwar South. There is strong evidence that the Department of Alabama St. Andrew's Cross "Cameron" flags were retained by the regiments in the Polk/Stuart Corps and the Cavalry Corps, if anything because they looked so much like the new thirteen-star flag.

The new flag, however, found no favor whatsoever with Maj. Gen. Pat Cleburne. One wonders if this Irishman disliked the Scottish heraldry this new flag to some extent displayed, or perhaps he remembered the several thousand of his own troops who fell in battle under the Hardee flag. He dissented so virulently that Johnston exempted his division's regiments from the order. New sets of blue Hardee colors were ordered, adorned with appropriate battle honors. Henceforth, Cleburne's Division was dubbed the "Blue Flag Division."

The newly issued flags differed from the earlier Hardee types in that the central disc now became a square with rounded corners. Additionally, the blue of the flags was lighter in field color and would lighten significantly in service.

Hand-scribed in black ink on the flag's field is a Union captor's legend: *"Captured with 17 officers and 165 men."* The fact that the writer documented his prize by writing on the field rather than the white border indicates how light the blue field must have been. The new flags might be referred to, with some justification, as the "Cleburne Issue."

Measuring approximately 31 x 38 inches, these battle flags were neither large nor ostentatious. They were battle flags in every sense of the word and would see many battles in 1864.

The illustrated flag of the combined Seventeenth and Eighteenth Dismounted Cavalry is one of those Cleburne Division issue flags. It served the regiment from early 1864 until summer, when it was captured around Atlanta in one of the many vicious engagements.

The battle honors, placed on the reverse of the flag prior to presentation to the regiment, document the major battles and actions in which the unit participated—Chickamauga, Tunnel Hill (the only bright spot in the Missionary Ridge debacle), and Ringgold Gap (a gallant rearguard stand by Cleburne's Division that saved the Army of Tennessee from destruction after the Missionary Ridge battle). These honors are mute testimony to the courage and fortitude of Cleburne's Texans, as well as the non-Texas regiments who fought with them.

Additionally, the regimental designation was colored-in with red and black ink. The ink bled through to the obverse side, which was blank—a common practice.

This flag survives today in the Texas State Archives. It is one of the few flags in the collection not in a state of suspended distress. Its blue field has faded to a light green, a common occurrence in Civil War flags with lighter blue pigments.

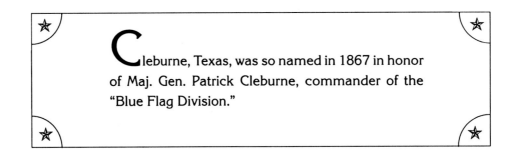

Cleburne, Texas, was so named in 1867 in honor of Maj. Gen. Patrick Cleburne, commander of the "Blue Flag Division."

Dimensions: 30" x 38" approx.

Sixth and Fifteenth Texas Infantry Regiment

Cleburne's Division, Franklin and Nashville

Replacement Type

Also exchanged after Arkansas Post, the subsequently combined Sixth and Fifteenth Texas Infantry Regiment (the Fifteenth being dismounted cavalry) was assigned to Cleburne's Division of Hardee's Corps, Army of Tennessee. Like the other Texas regiments, it would have an originally issued dark blue battle flag with a white oval-circular disc centered with a wide white border around the field. When Maj. Gen. Pat Cleburne's Division was granted exemption from Gen. Joe Johnston's new battle flag order, the Sixth and Fifteenth would have received a nearly identical flag as the one issued to the Seventeenth and Eighteenth Cavalry (Dismounted), probably displaying the very same battle honors. It is also probable that the Seventh Texas, as well as the Tenth Texas Infantry, received one. This made the possibility of four Texas regimental standards flying in Granbury's Texas Brigade, representing eight original Texas regiments.

By the end of the Atlanta Campaign in September 1864, the Sixth and Fifteenth's original Cleburne battle flag had been worn out by the constant fighting against Union General Sherman's invasion of the deep South. A new replacement battle flag was issued, similar but not identical to the lighter blue type issued to the regiment in the spring of 1864. This replacement issue flag featured a circular disc and no battle honors, although the lighter blue hue remained, as did the usual Hardee flag size of approximately 30 x 38 inches.

The illustration represents this replacement flag as it must have looked when first presented to the regiment. In the white disc was a tilted, nearly inverted Texas star. The bottom point was awkwardly pulled down, increasing the inverted effect. The blue color was apparently an appliquéd blue fabric. The lettering "TEXAS" surrounding the star, in the old Republic of Texas tradition, was embroidered in red. The regimental designation was embroidered in white.

When Gen. John B. Hood marched into Tennessee in a vain attempt to draw Sherman out of Georgia, the Sixth and Fifteenth Texas went with him. This flag flew over them during the last significant battles of the Army of Tennessee. It witnessed the violent deaths of Generals Cleburne and the Texan Granbury as they led the "Blue Flag" troops in a desperate charge against impregnable Union positions at Franklin. The flag was there to witness the crushing of the remnants of a once-magnificent Army of Tennessee by Union Gen. George Thomas' stronger Army of the Cumberland at Nashville.

This significant Texas regimental color lies today folded up in a small gray box in the Texas State Archives. Its light blue field has faded to a light green, and the embroidered lettering has faded to a colorless white. Only an outline of the star remains on the disc. Yet the flag still exists in a silent tribute to the hundreds of Texans who by then knew their cause was waning. That they fought on in the face of certain defeat is honor exhibited in the highest of Texas traditions.

This flag is one of the very few Texas unit battle flags that has received photographic coverage in a nationally distributed book, but it is unfortunately depicted upside down. Texas units are grossly underrepresented in such publications.

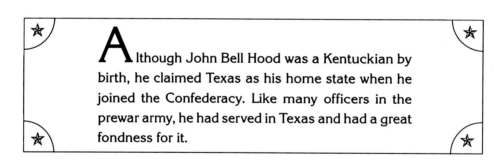

Although John Bell Hood was a Kentuckian by birth, he claimed Texas as his home state when he joined the Confederacy. Like many officers in the prewar army, he had served in Texas and had a great fondness for it.

Dimensions: 30" x 40"

Johnston Pattern Battle Flag
Army of Tennessee

Did any Texas units anywhere fight under this, the most recognized of Confederate flags today? Not a single flag of this type is known to have survived the war with a Texas unit affiliation. Only Texas units serving in the Central Confederacy in 1864 could have possibly used it. Historical evidence would tend to support the contention that Texas infantry and cavalry regiments associated with this army in 1864 used other flags.

The flag was adopted as the official battle flag of the Army of Tennessee by edict of Joe Johnston in the spring of 1864. Made in Atlanta, it was to gain lasting recognition because of the design's postwar adoption by the United Confederate Veterans and its later infamous use by white supremacist organizations that continues to this day.

In 1864 it was just a minor naval flag (the "jack") when adopted by Johnston, whose purpose in using this rectangular variant of the

Army of Northern Virginia's (ANV) battle flag was to end some of the confusion brought upon by the use of varied battle flags and to boost morale. His attempt was only partially successful. During the Atlanta Campaign, reinforcing units brought square flags similar to the ANV types and several units persisted in carrying the Second National Flag.

These were not the only exceptions. The most notable non-use of the Johnston flag was Brig. Gen. Patrick Cleburne's Division, which included Col. Hiram Granbury's Texas Brigade. Cleburne would have no part of the new flag, and with the permission of General Johnston the regiments of his division were issued a new, lighter blue Hardee-type flag of the type issued to the combined Seventeenth and Eighteenth Texas Cavalry (Dismounted) Regiment. Ross' Texas Cavalry Brigade, the Third, Sixth, Ninth, and Twenty-seventh regiments, had just received new twelve-starred Department of Alabama

(Cameron-manufactured) flags which were so very similar to the Johnston flags that apparently no change was made. That assumption is reinforced by the amount of wear shown on the three flags known to have survived the war. Terry's Texas Rangers did not receive a new flag. The Eleventh Texas Cavalry, like Terry's, served in such a detached manner that issue was also unlikely. Ector's Texas Brigade was also most likely issued the Department of Alabama type, but it is known that it ended the war in Alabama carrying the square ANV-type battle colors.

The best likelihood for a Texas unit carrying the Johnston flag is Good's/Douglas' Texas Battery, also known as the Dallas Light Artillery Company. This unit was the only Texas artillery to see significant service east of the Mississippi River. This battery of six (later four) cannon most probably fought in battles in 1862 and 1863, originally under a state or First National Flag. Later, the battery probably flew a dark blue Hardee flag until assigned to Hood's Corps of the Army of Tennessee in 1864. At this time, the battery (probably numbering fifty or sixty Tex-ans) was possibly issued a relatively small, 30 x 40-inch version of the Johnston Pattern Flag. The small flag was a pattern issue to field artillery in that army.

This active artillery unit served in the Army of Tennessee throughout the bloody battles of 1864. The battery ended its career defending Mobile, Alabama, in 1865. The use of the Johnston flag faded rapidly in late 1864 due to the loss of the manufacturing facility in Atlanta.

Infantry and cavalry flags of this type measured approximately 36 x 52 inches. It is probable the unit name and state designation were also placed on the flag with black battle honors inside the white fimbriation along the cross.

A Second National Flag in the Texas Confederate Museum, United Daughters of the Confederacy–Texas Division, has recently been associated with Good's-Douglas' Battery. As National-type battle flags were not unknown with the Army of Tennessee, the use of the Johnston flag even by the Texas battery can now be questioned.

Contrary to popular belief, there was never a "battle flag of the Confederacy" either by decree or use. The early Beauregard Pattern Battle Flag was approved only for the army in Virginia. The later white-bordered, square battle flags were common only in the Northeast Confederacy until late 1864–65, when they appeared in the Atlanta battles and subsequent coastal operations. The Johnston flag of 1864, erroneously called "The Confederate Battle Flag" or even "The Confederate Flag" today, has achieved fame far out of proportion to its use.

There is *no* flag that can lay claim to being the designated battle flag of the Confederacy.

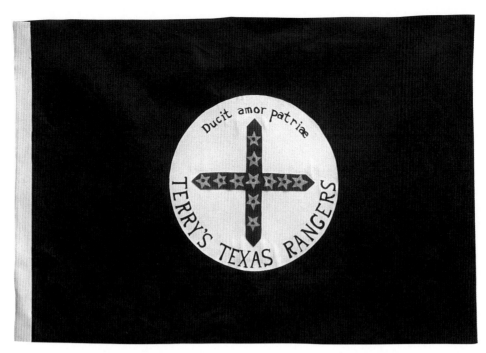

Dimensions: 28" x 43" approx.

Eighth Texas Cavalry Regiment/ Terry's Texas Rangers

September–October, 1864

The illustrated color is one of the two known flags of the Eighth Texas Volunteer Cavalry Regiment, Terry's Texas Rangers. It was presented to the regiment on September 20, 1864, but was only to see very short service. The color was lost to Union forces less than a month later, presumably having slipped off the staff while carried on horseback.[51]

This colorful banner was handmade from silk dresses by Misses Robbie Woodruff and Mary McIver, young ladies of Nashville, Tennessee.[52] The color is reminiscent of early war Hardee types, but also combines features of Polk Pattern Flags as well.

The reverse side replaced the regiment's motto "Ducit Amor Patriae" (loosely interpreted as "Sweet Love of Country") with "God Defend the Right" in English. The regimental name is on both sides of the central disc. A Union description (in which there are known errors) indicates that "the flag had a white and blue silk fringe with white and blue silk tassels."[53] The description mentioned a possible size of about 3 x 4 feet. A recently discovered line drawing in

the possession of the Victoria chapter of the United Daughters of the Confederacy–Texas records the flag as having a 28 x 43-inch field.

Upon receiving this flag, the Rangers retired the flag that they had used for two years.[54] The question is open as to what that flag was.

In 1898 the State of Indiana graciously returned this flag to Texas, preempting the federal government's return of captured Confederate flags by seven years. The flag was in the collection of the United Daughters of the Confederacy–Texas Division.[55][56] This historic flag has now been reported stolen.

The Eighth Texas Cavalry was involved in the last notable Confederate cavalry action of the war at Bentonville, South Carolina, on March 21, 1865. Along with the Fourth Tennessee Cavalry, it engaged in a rearguard charge to defend the remaining troops of Gen. Joe Johnston. At least one veteran indicated that the illustrated color was the last flag of Terry's Texas Rangers.[57]

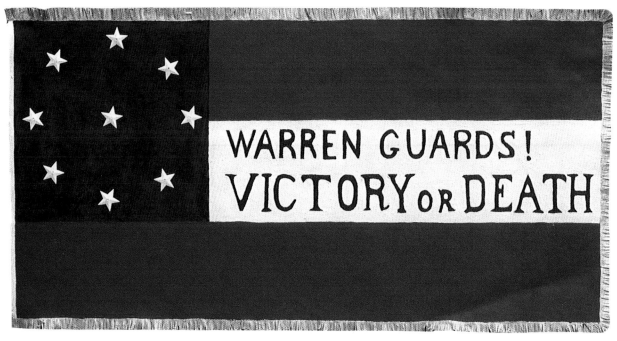

Dimensions: 4' x 8'

Warren Guards

First National Variant

Georgia, 1864

There may be some uncertainty about the capture details of this flag. It reputedly was seized by troops of Company K, Third Regiment, Ohio Volunteer Cavalry on October 13, 1864, near Rome, Georgia.[58] This color was reputedly associated with an unknown Texas unit, probably cavalry; hence the reason it was returned to Texas by its Federal captors. It may have been found in a supply wagon. Since Federal troops overran some positions and did capture pieces of artillery during their attack that day, wagons were probably taken in the process.

This First National Variant would probably have been a spare, left over from a time when flags were more plentiful. The unit name, "Warren Guards," indicates that it was probably a company flag originally. By this late date, however, it could have been a backup regimental color. The nine stars would indicate a manufacture date of sometime in mid-to-late 1861.

The unit name also suggests a possibility, if

not a probability, that this flag at least did not start out as a Texas color. Company names were often associated with counties. Although the record is incomplete, there is no known Texas unit named "Warren Guards." However, there was a "Warren Guards" from Warren County, Mississippi. The flag could very easily have originated from Vicksburg itself. Could the flag have eventually fallen into the possession of one of the many Texas units that operated in the Central Confederacy? The possibility cannot be discounted. National flags had a certain utility of purpose, and there is substantial evidence that "Stars and Bars" flags continued in use long after the Second National Flag was adopted.

This silk flag was large, measuring 4 x 8 feet. The gold-colored fringe was metallic gilt.[59] It is currently in the care of the Texas Confederate Museum, United Daughters of the Confederacy–Texas Division.

Dimensions: 38" x 52"

Twenty-sixth Texas Cavalry Regiment

Trans-Mississippi Department

A fairly typical example of a Texas-made St. Andrew's Cross type flag, this color features the large central star and unfimbriated blue cross on the red field. The red color of the flag's border is a bit unusual, as is the variance in width of the border along the top, bottom, and fly-edge, one and one-quarter inches respectively.[60] It is assumed that the borders of Texas-made Confederate flags were made from whatever color durable material was available to prevent fraying.

This flag measures 38 x 52 inches, so it had a more moderately rectangular look than many of the Texas St. Andrew's Cross types which tended to be of more square proportions. The field was made of challis while the cross, stars, and border were of cotton. The white canvas hoist edge featured twelve nail holes, a not too uncommon method of attachment.

This unit had a reputation for being very well trained. It was often referred to as "Debray's Texas Cavalry Regiment."

This flag is in the care of the Texas Confederate Museum, United Daughters of the Confederacy–Texas Division.

Sixteenth Texas Regiment

Company G

Trans-Mississippi Department

This flag is similar to the Fifth Texas Infantry's "Mary Young" flag. Made of cotton with silk stars, it measures 37 x 40 inches. Little is known about this color which, like so many of its sister Texas flags, lies in poor condition in a box at the Texas State Archives. A reference is attached linking it to "Company G, 16th Regiment," but there is no indication of cavalry or infantry (commonly referred to as volunteers). Both the Sixteenth Texas Volunteers (Infantry) and the Sixteenth Texas Cavalry Regiment served in Henry E. McCullough's Brigade. Additionally, the Seventeenth and Nineteenth Volunteers served in this brigade. The size of the flag was equally suitable for infantry or cavalry use. Texas cavalry units often did both as the need arose.

The large central star and lack of white fimbriation tend to indicate Texas origins. Other individual flags from units in other states sometimes display these features, but not with the consistency of Texas-produced flags.

These plain flags were effective and easy to make, giving them a certain utilitarian desirability.

Dimensions: 5' x 7'

Unknown Texas Regiment

Black Cross

St. Andrew's Cross Variant

This large, 5 x 7-foot cotton flag surrounded by a yellow border probably belonged to an infantry unit. Featuring a typical Texas-style unedged blue cross, this probable regimental color also displays a startling and unique black cross of unknown origin upon it. A white ribbon and small black retainer hang from the cross.

One possibility is that the cross and ribbon may have been a memorial to a popular fallen ranking officer. However, it is just as possible that the black cross was a postwar addition. It is unknown at this time if the cross covers a central thirteenth star. It will take a restoration expert to answer this question, as this flag lies folded up in a box at the Texas State Archives and due to its delicate condition cannot be examined by a layperson.

Flags of this style probably saw considerable service in West Louisiana and Arkansas.

Dimensions: 36" x 36" square

Unidentified Texas Regimental Flag

A striking example of Texas-produced flags with large stars is this unidentified banner. One explanation for the unusual feature is that this flag was made from a retired First National Variant, a perfectly logical, reasonable, and hopefully not-all-too-common practice. It is unconfirmed, but one corner of the St. Andrew's Cross may have featured a partial star in addition to the thirteen stars.

This 36 x 36-inch cotton battle flag exhibits the lack of white fimbriation along the blue cross. The field is bordered in white. It is suspected to have been the colors of the Sixth Texas Cavalry (Gould's Battalion), a Trans-Mississippi unit.[61]

This flag lies in a box at the Texas State Archives, unrestored and in poor condition. This is not the fault of the Archives' staff. They are responsible for thousands of archival relics and materials with totally inadequate resources. What little has been done with the flags was the result of a private grant which has long since been exhausted. Funding from the private sector is desperately needed to further preserve for our descendants these irreplaceable relics.

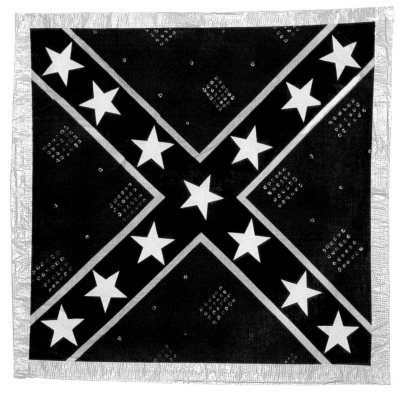

Dimensions: 32" x 32" square

Unidentified Texas Regimental Flag

Very similar but not identical to the Army of Northern Virginia's late bunting issue in overall design, this 32 x 32-inch square flag was made from a silk dress. A decorative pattern of yellow squares is displayed on the field. The white fimbriation on the blue cross and lack of a large central star are features not normally found on surviving Texas-made flags. Possibly a late-war flag, the variance should not be surprising considering the license exercised by individual civilian flag makers. Of course, there is also the possibility that this may not be a flag with Texas origins.

This battle flag is one of the few flags at the Texas State Archives to have received full restoration and preservation attention. It rests in an acrylic case in the storage facility.

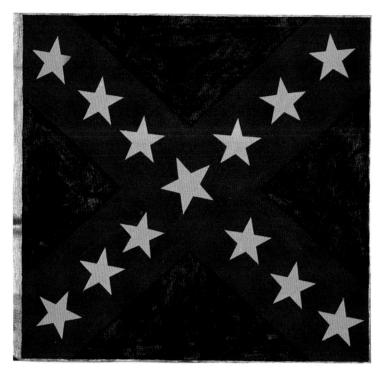

Dimensions: 6' x 6' square

Gen. Richard Taylor's Command

Western Louisiana Theater

The Taylor flag is a contradiction in colors. It features a red St. Andrew's Cross on a blue field, the reverse of the norm. It was probably used by some Texan and other Trans-Mississippi regiments in the Red River Campaign and at Pleasant Hill and Mansfield, Louisiana, in 1864. Approximately twenty-five Texas units of regimental strength comprised the majority of the forces defending western Louisiana. At least one regiment in this army used an upright red St. George's Cross in its flag similar to the Polk Pattern Flag. It can be speculated that perhaps the colors of the old Polk Corps' design inspired General Taylor to use a red cross instead of a regulation blue type. This is sheer speculation, of course. The example at the Texas State Archives shows Trans-Mississippi, possibly of Texas production origins, as the flag features the lack of white fimbriation on the red cross and a large central, tilted star.

Not all the regiments in Taylor's forces carried this type flag. Although the red-crossed flag has been associated with the western Louisiana theater, the forces here were, in many cases, dependent on their own resources. Any combination of Bonnie Blue, First and Second Nationals, St. Andrew's Cross, and unique flags might have been seen, but the red-crossed flags were probably dominant.

This silk flag, folded up in a box at the Texas State Archives, is bordered with a thick, gold-colored tape. Not depicted in the illustration are the small battle honors of Pleasant Hill and Mansfield located in the upper and lower quadrants. It measures a very large 6 x 6 feet square. It is not known if all the red cross flags were this large. It would seem unlikely.

A listing of the Texas units that served at Mansfield is provided in Appendix A.

Dimensions: 4' x 4' square approx.

Third Texas Infantry Regiment

Western Louisiana Theater

Presented to the regiment relatively late in the war while stationed at Shreveport, Louisiana, the Third Texas Infantry's flag indicates a certain preference in the western Louisiana theater for red-crossed dark blue flags. Made in silk by the women of Galveston, Texas, this superb regimental color was highlighted by the use of silver thread embroidery for the unit designation along with gold metallic fringe. So as to not make future generalizations easy, the Galveston women added white edging to the cross of this flag, which was somewhat atypical of most Texas-produced St. Andrew's Cross flags.

This battle flag measures approximately 4 x 4 feet square.[62] The hoist edge of the flag has been folded over to make a sleeve.

The Third Texas Infantry served primarily in coastal defense.

This flag rests in the care of the Texas Confederate Museum, United Daughters of the Confederacy–Texas Division. Silk flags are especially fragile and subject to aging. Funding is desperately needed to preserve the flags in the UDC and Texas Archives collections.

Dimensions: 4' x 4' square approx.

Ector's Texas Brigade

Fourth Bunting Issue

Central Confederacy

In June 1864 the Richmond Clothing Depot initiated a new issue of flags that to some extent began replacing the Third Bunting Issue in the Army of Northern Virginia. A few inches larger, the Fourth Bunting Issue featured larger stars spaced out more evenly and a somewhat larger St. Andrew's Cross. It is certainly possible that the First, Fourth, and Fifth Texas infantry regiments of the ANV used this type late in the war.

Ector's Texas Brigade of the Army of Tennessee through some source received four of this style flag either in late 1864 or early 1865, perhaps after being assigned detached service from Hood's Army of Tennessee.[63] Ector's Texas Brigade included the Fourteenth, Tenth, and eventually the Thirty-second Texas Cavalry (Dismounted) Regiments, as well as Maxey's Ninth Texas Infantry. The regiments in this brigade fought under many different types of battle flags during their Civil War careers.

Ector's Brigade was captured on April 9, 1865, at Spanish Fort, Alabama, after being overwhelmed by superior Union forces.[64] Supposedly the flags of the Eleventh, Fourteenth, and Tenth Texas Cavalry (Dismounted) Regiments were seized by Federal troops, but a soldier of the Ninth Texas smuggled his regiment's colors home.

Some question arises as to whether the Eleventh Texas Cavalry ever served with the brigade. It is possible an error was made in identifying this regiment's number. The color could have belonged to the Thirty-second Texas Cavalry, which was at this post.

The captured wool flags measured slightly larger that 4 x 4 feet square.

Dimensions: 11½" x 20½"

Lone Star Guidon

This swallowtail cavalry guidon was seized in action or confiscated by Federal troops in 1865 at "Miriam" (Milam), Texas, after hostilities had ceased. This banner was most probably a cavalry guidon, as its size (11½ x 20½ inches exclusive of fringe) would have made it useless to infantry or artillery.[65]

It might be worthwhile to point out that when Union troops occupied Texas there were Texans who, through bitterness, poverty, frustration, or a combination of several factors, engaged in terroristic assaults against Union forces, recently freed slaves, and the overwhelming majority of Texans who stoically and courageously accepted the verdict of force imposed upon them.

Texas was still a rural wilderness after the war, and policing its vast expanses was difficult for Federal forces. The possession of Confederate uniforms, flags, and the like was prohibited, and these articles were seized whenever possible to discourage any lingering Confederate sympathies. It is a credit to those Texan families who, despite the risk, held on to and cherished these personal mementos and icons of Texas' Civil War history.

Dimensions: 34" x 42"

Unidentified Texas Unit Flag

St. Andrew's Cross Variant

Troops from the 15th Maine Infantry Regiment seized this flag while in Texas.[66] This St. Andrew's Cross variant type battle flag is uncommon because of its star pattern placed in the field rather than on the arms of the blue cross. This flag also presents a plain blue cross with unfimbriated edges, so typical of Texas-style colors in this particular type.

The flag measures a moderate 34 x 42 inches. This cotton banner could have been a company or a regimental type flag.[67]

Although unusual, this color is not entirely unique. A unit known as Robertson's Cavaliers also used a flag of similar design and features including the stars on the field instead of the cross. The star pattern on the field is a little different and the flag has a yellow fringe.

The flags are so similar, they might have belonged to companies in the same regiment or regiments in the same brigade. The flag is in the care of the Texas Confederate Museum, United Daughters of the Confederacy–Texas Division.

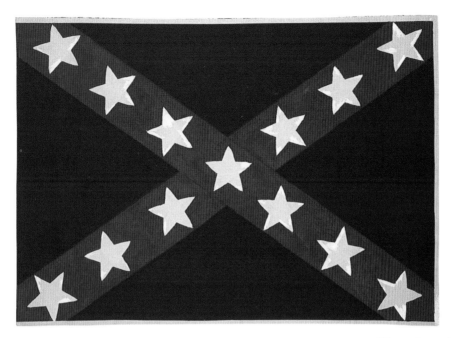

Dimensions: 4' x 6'

Unidentified Texas Unit Flag

(Unofficial Naval Ensign?)

This cotton flag, in very tattered condition, was donated to the Texas Confederate Museum in June 1968. It was purported to be a naval ensign flown during the Battle of Brownsville in 1865. There was no such official action, but the Battle of Palmetto Ranch (also referred to as "Palmito") was fought near Brownsville, on May 13, 1865. This engagement was the last land battle of the Civil War.

Perhaps this flag is a relic of that historic fight. If so, could it have been a naval jack or an unofficial naval ensign borrowed from a small Confederate vessel? Could it have been used by a small contingent of Confederate sailors during the battle? Anything is possible.

Of course, the official naval ensigns were the First and Second National Flags of the Confederate States of America. For example, the ironclad *Merrimac* (actually C.S.S. *Virginia*) carried a Stars and Bars (First National) on its stern when it engaged the Union *Monitor*. The famous raider C.S.S. *Alabama*, when cornered by the Union's *Kearsarge*, flew the Second National

Flag (as did the raider *Florida*, taken illegally in a neutral port). The raider *Shenandoah*, the last Confederate vessel to surrender to Union forces, flew the Second National Flag as it decimated the U.S. Pacific whaling fleet.

The Rosenberg Library in Galveston possesses two Confederate naval flags. One, which was flown on the Confederate schooner *Dart*, is a classic First National type design. The other, of the Confederate *Royal Yacht*, appears to be a converted U.S. Navy jack. It is dark blue with sixteen white stars in a square pattern surrounding a seventeenth white star appliquéd on to a dark square of additional dark blue material.

The term "ensign" must not be used too loosely. However, the illustrated flag's use as an unofficial ensign cannot be discounted. Its size, approximately 4 x 6 feet, could have made it suitable for that purpose. The lack of white fimbriation on the blue cross would seem to suggest this flag had Texas origins.[68]

This flag is in the Texas Confederate Museum, Daughters of the Confederacy–Texas.

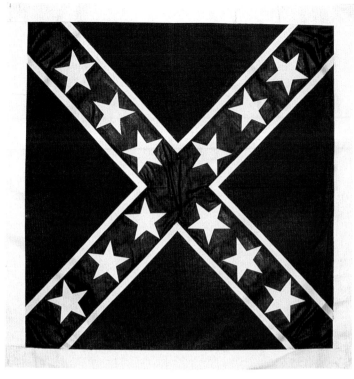

Dimensions: 5½' x 5½' square

First Texas Infantry Regiment

Last Flag

Army of Northern Virginia
Richmond Clothing Depot

The Richmond Clothing Depot, Richmond, Virginia, issued replacement flags to regiments as needed. The flag illustrated here is a twelve-star type and has been documented to have begun use as early as September 1864 (issued to a Virginia regiment). Of note regarding this type of ANV regimental variant are the larger stars, the missing thirteenth star, and the slightly more air-spaced star pattern. Aside from these differences, the flag is generally similar to the "Third Bunting Issue."

This particular color was returned to Texas in 1905 and was documented in the booklet "The Returned Battle Flags," a color pamphlet published by the Cotton Belt Railroad Co. for the June 14, 1905, Confederate Veterans' Reunion in Louisville, Kentucky. It was referred to as "the battle flag of the First Texas Infantry Regiment captured at the battle of Appomattox, April 8, 1865."[69] This author did not locate this flag in the Texas State Archives collection, nor has it been confirmed to be in the United Daughters of the Confederacy collection. Fortunately, identical types have survived in Virginia to give us historical confirmation.

This flag reputedly measures approximately 5½ feet square.

Texas Units at Mansfield
Richard Taylor's Forces
Trans-Mississippi Department

Texas Cavalry	Texas Infantry*
Fourth	Eleventh
Fifth	Twelfth
Seventh	Fifteenth
Thirteenth Battalion	Sixteenth
First Texas Partisans	Seventeenth
Second Texas Partisans	Eighteenth
First	Nineteenth
Twenty-sixth	Twenty-second
Thirty-fourth	Sixth Cavalry
	Thirteenth Cavalry
	Twenty-eighth Cavalry
	Thirty-first Cavalry

* Including Dismounted Cavalry

Source: *Official Records*, Series I, Vol. 34, Pt. 1, p. 563 cf.;
Vol. 26, Pt. 2, pp. 402, 465; Vol. 41, Pt. 3, pp. 966–971.

A Synoptic Table of Events in the War Between the States*

Preliminary Events

December 1860
20th: South Carolina Convention adopts Ordinance of Secession.
26th: United States garrison of Charleston Harbor moved from Ft. Moultrie to Ft. Sumter.

January 1861
9th: U.S. steamer *Star of the West* bringing reinforcements to Ft. Sumter fired on by South Carolina state troops. Mississippi State Convention adopts Ordinance of Secession.
10th: Florida State Convention adopts Ordinance of Secession. U.S. garrison of Pensacola Harbor moved to Ft. Pickens.
11th: Alabama State Convention adopts Ordinance of Secession.
19th: Georgia State Convention adopts Ordinance of Secession.
24th: Referendum vote in North Carolina against calling State Convention.
26th: Louisiana State Convention adopts Ordinance of Secession.

February 1861
1st: **Texas State Convention adopts Ordinance of Secession.**
4th: Provisional government of Confederate States of America organized in Montgomery, Alabama. Peace Convention called by Virginia; met in Washington, D.C.
9th: Hon. Jefferson Davis elected provisional

president, and Alexander Stevens, vice president of Confederate States of America. Referendum vote in Tennessee against calling State Convention.
13th: Virginia State Convention meets.
18th: Confederate provisional officers inaugurated in Montgomery, Alabama.

March 1861
4th: Abraham Lincoln inaugurated president of the United States; Confederate Provisional Congress of CSA adopts and flies for the first time the Stars and Bars in answer to Lincoln's inauguration; Arkansas State Convention defeats Ordinance of Secession.
11th: Constitution of the Confederate States adopted by Congress.
16th: Confederate Congress adjourned.

April 1861
11th: Final demand by Confederate government for surrender of Ft. Sumter.
12th & 13th: **Bombardment of Ft. Sumter begins by Confederate batteries under CSA Gen. P. G. T. Beauregard.**
14th: Ft. Sumter evacuated.
15th: President Lincoln calls for troops to be sent against seceding states.
17th: Virginia State Convention submits Ordinance of Secession to referendum vote.
19th: President Lincoln declares blockade of

---

* Source: From the classic *The Story of the Confederacy* by Robert Selph Henry (Bobbs-Merill, 1931. Reprinted 1989. New York: Del Capo/Plenum Publishing.) Special permission for printing this excerpt has been graciously granted by Mrs. Robert Selph Henry.

Confederate ports.

24th: Virginia enters into military alliance with Confederate States of America.

29th: Confederate Provisional Congress meets in Montgomery, Alabama, at called session.

May 1861

6th: Arkansas State Convention adopts Ordinance of Secession.

7th: Tennessee legislature submits Ordinance of Secession to referendum vote; votes military alliance with Confederate States of America.

10th & 11th: Missouri militia at Camp Jackson, St. Louis, seized by Union forces, followed by rioting in city.

13th: Delegates elected to North Carolina State Convention. Baltimore seized by Gen. B. F. Butler's troops.

20th: North Carolina State Convention adopts Ordinance of Secession.

21st: Confederate Congress adjourned; to meet again in Richmond, Virginia.

23rd: Virginia voters ratify Ordinance of Secession.

24th: Union troops enter Virginia.

29th: Capital of Confederate States of America transferred to Richmond, Virginia; executive departments to be transferred during June.

June 1861

1st: Capt. John Q. Marr, Warrenton Rifles, killed in skirmish at Fairfax Courthouse — first Confederate battle death.

8th: Tennessee election ratifies Ordinance of Secession. Gen. S. B. Buckner, commanding Kentucky state forces, enters into neutrality agreements with Union General McClelland and Governor Harris of Tennessee.

OPERATIONS IN VIRGINIA	OPERATIONS IN CEN. SOUTH	OPERATIONS IN MISS. VALLEY	COASTAL & WESTERN OPERATIONS
JUNE 1861			
3rd: CSA outposts defeated at Philippi, WV *10th:* Union advance repulsed at Big Bethel, VA *17th:* Union reconnaisance defeated at Vienna, VA		*17th:* Missouri state troops defeated by Union General Lyon at Booneville, MO	
JULY 1861			
11th: CSA forces driven from Rich Mntn, WV *13th:* Engagement at Carrick's Ford, WV *17th:* Skirmish at Scarey Creek, WV *18th:* Union force repulsed at Blackburn's Ford, VA (Bull Run) *20th:* Confederate Provisional Congress convenes at Richmond, VA *21st: Battle of Manassas, VA*		*5th to 26th:* Engagements between Missouri state troops and Union Army at: Carthage, 5th; Millsville, 16th; Fulton & Martinsburg, 17th; Monroe Sta., 19th; Forsythe, 22nd; Blue Mills, 24th; Lane's Prairie, 26th	**27th: Ft. Fillmore, San Augustine Springs, NM, and garrison captured by CSA Texas forces under Baylor**

A Synoptic Table of Events in the War Between the States (contd.)

OPERATIONS IN VIRGINIA	OPERATIONS IN CEN. SOUTH	OPERATIONS IN MISS. VALLEY	COASTAL & WESTERN OPERATIONS
		AUGUST 1861	
26th: Engagement at Cross Lane or Summerville, WV **31st:** Confederate Congress ends session at Richmond	**6th:** Camp Dick Robinson, KY established by the Unionists	**10th:** Battle of Wilson's Creek, MO, also called Oak Hill or Springfield; General Lyon killed **2nd - 9th:** Engagements between Union and Missouri state troops at: Dug Springs, 2nd; Athens, 5th; Brunswick, 17th; Charleston, 19th	**29th:** Fort Hatteras, NC and Hatteras Inlet seized by Union navy & army
		SEPTEMBER 1861	
10th: Engagement at Carnifex Ferry, WV **12th & 13th:** CSA attack on Cheat Mtn., WV, fails **25th:** Engagement at Kanawah Gap, WV		**3rd:** CSA forces under Polk occupy Columbus, KY **4th:** Union forces under Grant occupy Paducah, KY **12th-20th:** Missouri state troops besiege and capture Lexington, MO	**17th:** Union navy captures Ship Island, MS
		OCTOBER 1861	
3rd: Engagement at Greenbriar, WV **16th:** Skirmish at Bolivar Hts., VA **21st:** Union repulsed at Ball's Bluff, VA, near Leesburg		**13th-25th:** Engagements between Missouri state forces and Fremont's Union troops in Missouri at: Monday's Hollow, 13th; Underwood's Farm, 14th; Potosi, 15th; Ironton, 17th-21st; Springfield, 25th **31st:** "Rebel Legislature" of Missouri at Neosho votes to secede	**9th:** CSA attacks Santa Rosa Island, Pensacola, FL

A Synoptic Table of Events in the War Between the States (contd.)

OPERATIONS IN VIRGINIA	OPERATIONS IN CEN. SOUTH	OPERATIONS IN MISS. VALLEY	COASTAL & WESTERN OPERATIONS
NOVEMBER 1861			
12th: Outpost skirmish at Pohick, Church, VA *18th:* Confederate Provisional Congress meets *26th:* Cavalry skirmish at Dranesville, VA	*9th:* Skirmish at Ivy Mountain, KY *18th:* Kentucky State Convention at Russellville votes to secede amd join the Confederate States; new governor elected	*7th:* Grant repulsed from Belmont, MO, by CSA troops under Gens. Pillow and Polk	*7th:* Capture of Port Royal Harbor and Hilton Head Island by Union fleet & army *8th:* CSA Commissioners Mason and Slidell taken from British *Trent* in Bahama Channel *23rd:* CSA attacks Ft. Pickens at Pensacola, FL, repulsed
DECEMBER 1861			
13th: Engagement at Buffalo Mountain, WV *20th:* Engagement at Dranesville, VA	*17th:* Skirmish at Rowlett's Station, KY *28th:* Cavalry skirmish at Sacramenton, KY	*3rd-28th:* Engagements between Missouri state forces and Union troops at: Salem, 3rd; Milford, 18th; Mt. Zion and Hallville, 28th	
JANUARY 1862			
4th: Bath, VA, captured by CSA forces	*10th:* Engagement at Middle Creek, Paintsville, KY *19th & 20th:* Union army defeats CSA forces at Mill Springs and Logan's Cross Roads, KY	*8th:* Cavalry skirmish at Charleston, MO	*1st:* CSA Commissioners Mason and Slidell released

A Synoptic Table of Events in the War Between the States (contd.)

Operations in Virginia	Operations in Cen. South	Operations in Miss. Valley	Coastal & Western Operations
February 1862			
17th: Confederate Provisional Congress adjourns *18th:* Confederate Regular Congress meets *22nd:* Confederate "permanent" government inaugurated at Richmond, VA	*6th:* Ft. Henry, TN, captured by Union navy gunboats *16th:* Ft. Donelson, TN, and garrison captured by Union navy and gunboats *23rd:* Nashville, TN, occupied by Union army; Southern Kentucky and Middle Tennessee lost to Confederacy	*17th:* Skirmish at Sugar Creek, AR *20th:* CSA fortifications at Columbus, KY, evacuated	*8th:* CSA fortifications at Roanoke Island, NC, and garrison captured by Union fleet and army *10th:* CSA "Mosquito Fleet" destroyed at Elizabeth City, NC *21st:* CSA victory at Valverde, NM *28th:* CSA cruiser *Nashville* destroyed
March 1862			
8th: C.S.S. *Virginia* sinks U.S.S. *Cumberland* and *Congress* off Hampton Roads, VA *9th:* Battle between ironclads CSA *Virginia (Merrimac)* and Union *Monitor* *20th:* CSA army repulsed at Kernstown, VA	*8th:* Col. J.H. Morgan's Cavalry raids suburbs of Nashville, TN	*1st:* Grant's Union army begins concentration at Pittsburg Landing (Shiloh), TN; CSA Gen. A.S. Johnston's forces at Corinth, MS *6th, 7th & 8th:* CSA defeat at Elk Horn Tavern (Pea Ridge), AR *13th & 14th:* New Madrid, MO, captured by Union troops	*14th:* New Bern, NC, captured by Union troops *26th, 27th and 28th:* Engagement at Glorieta Pass near Santa Fe, NM; CSA retreat begun to Texas
April 1862			
4th: Union Gen. McLelland's siege of Yorktown, VA, begun *21st:* Confederate Congress adjourned after passing Conscription Act	*12th:* Union raiders capture engine *General*; recaptured by CSA using engine *Texas* *29th:* Union troops, advancing east from Huntsville, capture Bridgeport, AL	*6th:* **Battle of Shiloh, TN:** CSA under Johnston and Beauregard win first day *7th:* Union troops under Grant and Buell defeat CSA second day *8th:* CSA fortifications and garrison on Island No. 10 in Mississippi River surrendered *18th:* Union navy bombards CSA Fts. St. Philip and Jackson guarding New Orleans *24th:* Union Admiral Farragut's fleet captures New Orleans, LA *28th:* Union General Halleck opens Siege of Corinth, MS	*11th:* CSA Ft. Pulaski, GA, at mouth of Savannah River captured by Union troops *25th:* Ft. Macon, NC, captured by Union troops

A Synoptic Table of Events in the War Between the States (contd.)

Operations In Virginia	Operations In Cen. South	Operations In Miss. Valley	Coastal & Western Operations
May 1862			
4th: CSA Yorktown, VA, evacuated; **CSA Gen. T.J. "Stonewall" Jackson opens first Shenandoah Valley Campaign** *5th:* Battle of Williamsburg, VA *7th:* Engagement at Etham's Landing, VA *8th:* Engagement at McDowell, VA *9th:* CSA Norfolk, VA, evacuated *11th:* CSA destroys *Virginia* *15th:* Union navy advances up the James River, repulsed at Drewry's Bluff, VA *23rd:* Jackson defeats Banks at Front Royal, VA *24th to 30th:* Jackson drives Banks from Shenandoah Valley; engagements at Middletown, 24th; Newtown, 24th; Winchester, 25th; Charlestown, 28th *27th:* Battle of Hanover Court House, VA *30th:* Skirmish at Front Royal, VA *31st to June 1st:* **Battle of Seven Pines (Fair Oaks), VA; CSA Gen. J.E. Johnston wounded; Gen. Robert E. Lee takes command**	*5th:* CSA Col. J.H. Morgan's Cavalry defeated at Lebanon, TN	*19th:* Cavalry skirmish at Searcy Landing, AR *29th & 30th:* CSA Corinth, MS, evacuated by Gen. P.G.T. Beauregard; Union siege lifted	*10th:* CSA Pensacola, FL, evacuated and occupied by Union troops
June 1862			
1st: Close of Battle of Seven Pines, VA *6th:* Engagement at Harrisonburg, VA, as CSA General Jackson retreats; Col. T. Ashby killed *8th:* Battle of Cross Keys, VA *9th:* Battle of Port Republic, VA *11th to 14th:* Stuart's Raid around Union General McClelland's army *26th to July 1st:* **The Seven Days Battles begin**	*18th:* Cumberland Gap, TN, evacuated; occupied by Union forces	*4th:* CSA Ft. Pillow, TN, evacuated *6th:* Memphis, TN, occupied after destruction of CSA river fleet *17th:* Gunboat battle at St. Charles, White River, AR *26th to 29th:* Farragut's Union fleet passes CSA Vicksburg, MS, batteries, joins Union upper river fleet	*10th:* Skirmish at James Island near Charleston, NC *16th:* Union advance on Charleston repulsed at Secessionville, SC

A Synoptic Table of Events in the War Between the States (contd.)

Operations In Virginia	Operations In Cen. South	Operations In Miss. Valley	Coastal & Western Operations
	JULY 1862		
26 June–July 1st: The Seven Days Battle; Battles around Richmond, VA: Mechanicsville, 26th; Gaine's Mill, 27th; Golding's Farm, 28th; Savage Station, 29th; Frayser's Farm, 30th ***1st:*** Battle of Malvern Hill, VA; followed by establishment of new Union base on James River at Harrison Landing	***4th to 28th:*** CSA Col. J.H. Morgan's first Kentucky Raid; engagements at Tomkinsville, 9th; Lebanon, 12th; Cynthiana, 17th; Gallatin, TN, 21st ***13th:*** Capture of Murfreesboro, TN, and Union garrison by Gen. N.B. Forrest	***7th:*** Engagement at Bayou Cache (Cotton Plant), AR ***15th:*** Naval engagement near Vicksburg, MS; CSA ram *Arkansas* vs. Union fleet	
	AUGUST 1862		
9th: Battle of Cedar Mountain; Union repulse ***18th:*** Session of Confederate Congress opens ***23rd to Sept 1st: Second Manassas (Bull Run) Campaign,*** with skirmishes on the Rappahannock River, 23rd. to 25th. Engagements at Bull Run Bridge, 27th; Groveton, 28th; Gainesville, 29th **Battle of Second Manassas, 30th**	***12th:*** Union garrison at Gallatin, TN, captured by Morgan ***23rd:*** Skirmish at Big Hill, KY ***28th:*** CSA General Bragg marches out of Chattanooga, TN, on Kentucky Campaign ***30th:*** Battle of Richmond, KY, won by CSA General Kirby Smith's troops	***5th:*** CSA attempt to recapture Baton Rouge, LA, repulsed by Union troops and navy ***6th to 16th:*** Cavalry engagements in Missouri at Kirksville, 6th; Independence, 11th; Lone Jack, 16th	***24th:*** CSA cruiser *Alabama* commissioned at sea off the Azores in the Atlantic Ocean

A Synoptic Table of Events in the War Between the States (contd.)

OPERATIONS IN VIRGINIA	OPERATIONS IN CEN. SOUTH	OPERATIONS IN MISS. VALLEY	COASTAL & WESTERN OPERATIONS
SEPTEMBER 1862			
1st: Battle of Chantilly (Ox Hill), VA *5th:* Lee crosses Potomac River into Maryland *10th:* Engagement at Fayetteville, WV *12th to 15th:* CSA capture of Harper's Ferry, by Jackson *14th:* Battles of Boonsboro and Crampton's Gap, South Mountain, MD *16th & 17th:* **Battle of Sharpsburg, (Antietam), MD** *19th:* Lee crosses into Virginia *20th:* Engagement at Shepherds-town, VA *22nd:* Lincoln issues Emancipation Proclamation	*16th:* Bragg captures Munfordville, KY *19th:* Bragg marches toward Frankfort, KY	*19th & 20th:* CSA General Price repulsed at Battle of Iuka, MS *30th:* CSA driven from Missouri in engagement at Newtonia	*6th:* Engagement at Washington, NC
OCTOBER 1862			
1st: Cavalry engagement at Shepherdstown, VA; Stuart's first Pennsylvania cavalry raid *13th:* CSA Congress adjourns *26th:* McClelland crosses Potomac into Virginia	*4th:* Richard Hawes inaugurated Confederate governor of Kentucky *8th:* Battle of Perryville, KY *10th:* Engagement at Harrodsburg, KY *17th:* Cavalry skirmish at Lexington, KY	*3rd & 4th:* CSA attack by Generals Van Dorn and Price at Corinth, MS, repulsed *5th:* Rear guard action at Big Hatchie, MS	*22nd:* Union attacks Pocotaligo (or Yemassee), SC; repulsed
NOVEMBER 1862			
1st to 5th: Cavalry skirmishes at Philomont, Bloomfield, Union, Barbee's Cross Roads and Chester Gap, VA *28th:* Cavalry skirmish at Hartwood Church, VA		*7th:* Engagement at Mariana, AR *8th:* Engagement at Hudsonville, MS *28th:* CSA repulsed at Boston Mtn. (Cane Hill), AR	

A Synoptic Table of Events in the War Between the States (contd.)

OPERATIONS IN VIRGINIA	OPERATIONS IN CEN. SOUTH	OPERATIONS IN MISS. VALLEY	COASTAL & WESTERN OPERATIONS
DECEMBER 1862			
13th: Union repulse at Battle of Fredericksburg, VA *27th:* Cavalry skirmish at Dumfries, VA	*7th:* Morgan captured Hartsville, TN and garrison *25th to 28th:* Morgan's "Christmas Raid" to Kentucky, with engagements at Green's Chapel, 25th; Bacon Creek, 26th; Elizabethtown, 27th; Bacon Creek, 28th *30th:* Engagement at Watauga Bridge and Carter's Station, TN *31st to January 2nd:* Battle of Stone's River, TN	*7th:* Battle of Prairie Grove, near Fayetteville, AR *16th to January 1st:* Forrest's first West Tennessee raid, with engagements at Lexington, 18th; Jackson, 19th; Trenton, 20th; Parker's Cross Roads, 30th *20th:* Grant's advanced base at Holly Spring, MS, destroyed by Van Dorn *28th and 29th:* Sherman's attack on Chickasaw Bayou, Vicksburg, MS, repulsed	*12th to 18th:* Union expedition to Goldsboro, NC, repulsed
JANUARY 1863			
12th: Confederate Congress meets *30th:* Skirmish at Deserted House, near Suffolk, VA	*3rd:* Bragg withdraws from Murfreesboro to Tullahoma, TN *24th:* Skirmish at Woodbury, TN	*11th:* Ft. Hindman, at Arkansas Post, captured by Union troops and gunboats *14th:* Land and water engagement at Bayou Teche, LA	*1st:* Recapture of Galveston, TX, by Magruder *11th: Alabama* sinks *Hatteras* *15th:* Confederate cruiser *Florida* sails from Mobile *31st:* Raid of Confederate gunboats *Chicora* and *Palmetto State* on blockading fleet off Charleston Harbor
FEBRUARY 1863			
	3rd: Confederate attack on Ft. Donelson driven off		

A Synoptic Table of Events in the War Between the States (contd.)

OPERATIONS IN VIRGINIA	OPERATIONS IN CEN. SOUTH	OPERATIONS IN MISS. VALLEY	COASTAL & WESTERN OPERATIONS
MARCH 1863			
8th: CSA Colonel Mosby's midnight raid on Fairfax Court House, and capture of General Stoughman *17th:* Cavalry engagement at Kelly's Ford, VA	*4th & 5th:* Engagement at Thompson's Station, TN *20th:* Engagement at Vaught's Hill, near Milton, TN *25th:* Forrest's raid on Brentwood and Franklin, TN *22nd to Apr. 1st:* Cluke's (of Morgan's Cavalry) raid in Kentucky, with engagements at Mt. Sterling, 22nd; Danville, 24th; Dutton's Hill, 30th	*13th to Apr. 5th:* Union gunboats and army repulsed at Ft. Pemberton, attempting Yazoo River approach to Vicksburg *14th:* Farragut's Union fleet runs past CSA batteries at Port Hudson *16th to 22nd:* Union attempt to reach Vicksburg by gunboat via Steele's Bayou repulsed *28th:* Engagement at Pattersonville, LA, between Taylor's CSA forces and Union gunboats	
APRIL 1863			
12th to May 4th: Siege of Suffolk, VA, by Longstreet's CSA forces *27th to May 8th:* Stoneman's Union cavalry raid in Virginia	*2nd & 3rd:* Cavalry skirmish at Woodbury and Snow Hill, TN *10th:* CSA cavalry attack on Franklin, TN *27th to May 3rd:* Streight's Union cavalry raid to Rome, GA; captured by Gen. N.B. Forrest	*12th to 14th:* Engagement at Bisland, LA *17th to May 2nd:* Grierson's Union cavalry raid from La Grange, TN, to Baton Rouge, LA *26th:* Union repulse of Marmaduke's cavalry at Cape Girardeau, MO *27th:* Union gunboat fleet attack on Grand Gulf, MS, repulsed	*1st:* Cruiser C.S.S. *Georgia* commissioned *7th:* Union navy ironclad attack on Ft. Sumter repulsed; one monitor sunk

A Synoptic Table of Events in the War Between the States (contd.)

Operations in Virginia	Operations in Cen. South	Operations in Miss. Valley	Coastal & Western Operations
		MAY 1863	
1st to 4th: Battle of Chancellorsville, VA; Lt. Gen. T.J. "Stonewall" Jackson mortally wounded; Battles at Fredricksburg and Salem Church on same day **1st:** Confederate Congress adjourns **4th:** CSA Lieutenant General Longstreet raises siege of Norfolk, VA		**1st:** Grant captures Port Gibson, below Vicksburg **12th:** CSA defeat at Battle of Raymond, MS **14th:** Grant captures Jackson, MS **16th:** Union victory at Champion's Hill, MS **17th:** CSA driven across Big Black River, MS **18th to July 4th: Grant opens siege of Vicksburg, MS** **23rd to July 8th:** Siege of Port Hudson, LA	
		JUNE 1863	
9th: Cavalry battles at Brandy Station and Beverly Ford, VA **13th and 15th:** Second battle of Winchester, VA; much of town and Union garrison captured by CSA General Ewell **17th:** Cavalry fight at Aldie, VA **21st:** Cavalry fight at Upperville, VA **30th:** Cavalry fight at Hanover, PA	**4th:** CSA demonstration against Franklin, TN **9th:** Cavalry skirmish at Monticello, KY **16th:** Cavalry skirmish at Triplett's Bridge, TN **23rd to July 7th:** Union Gen. Rosecrans' Tullahoma Campaign, flanking Bragg out of his Middle Tennessee positions, to fall back to Chattanooga	**1st to 30th: Siege of Vicksburg and of Port Hudson** **6th to 8th:** Taylor's attack on Milliken's Bend, LA, repulsed **20th & 21st:** Engagement at La Fourche Crossing, LA **23rd:** Attack on Union garrison at Brashear City, LA **28th:** Taylor's attack on Donaldsonville, LA	**17th:** CSA gunboat *Atlanta* captured in Wassaw Sound, GA

A Synoptic Table of Events in the War Between the States (contd.)

Operations In Virginia	Operations In Cen. South	Operations In Miss. Valley	Coastal & Western Operations
JULY 1863			
1st to 3rd: **Battle of Gettysburg** *4th & 5th:* Cavalry fights at Monterey Gap and Fairfield, PA; Smithsburg, MD *6th:* Cavalry fights at Hagerstown and Williamsport, MD *7th to 9th:* Cavalry fight at Boonsboro, MD *10th:* Rear-guard action at Falling Waters, MD *16th:* Rear-guard action at Shepherdstown, VA *17th:* Cavalry fight at Wytheville, VA *21st to 23rd:* Cavalry fights at Manassas Gap and Chester Gap, in Blue Ridge Mountains, VA	*2nd to 26th:* Morgan's raid into Kentucky, Indiana and Ohio, with engagements at Lebanon, KY 5th; Buffington Bar, OH, 19th; Beaver Creek, OH, 26th *14th:* Rear-guard action at Elk River, TN	*4th:* **Vicksburg surrendered;** CSA attempt to recapture Helena, AR, repulsed *5th:* Engagements at Bolton and Birdsong Ferry, MS *8th:* Port Hudson, LA, surrendered *9th to 16th:* Sherman's campaign against Gen. J.E. Johnston; Jackson, MS, reoccupied by Union troops *13th:* Yazoo City, MS, captured; engagement at Donaldsonville, LA	*10th to Sept 6th:* Siege of Fort Wagner, Morris Island, Charleston Harbor, with bombardment of Ft. Sumter and the city *17th:* Cavalry engagement at Honey Springs, Indian Territory
AUGUST 1863			
1st to 3rd: Cavalry battles at Rappahannock Station, Brandy Station, and Kelly's Ford, VA *26th and 27th:* Engagement at Rocky Gap, near White Sulphur Springs, WV			*1st to 31st:* Union bombardment of Ft. Wagner and Ft. Sumter, SC
SEPTEMBER 1863			
13th: Cavalry fight at Culpeper, VA *19th:* Cavalry fight at Rockville, MD	*9th:* Cumberland Gap, TN, and CSA garrison captured; Bragg evacuates Chattanooga, TN *19th and 20th:* **Battle of Chickamauga, TN;** Rosencrans retreats to Chattanooga	*10th:* CSA Little Rock, AR, evacuated *27th to Oct 28th:* CSA Col. Joe Shelby's cavalry raid into MO	*6th:* Ft. Wagner, SC, evacuated *8th:* Union attack on Sabine Pass, TX, repulsed *10th:* Night attack on Ft. Sumter, SC, repulsed

A Synoptic Table of Events in the War Between the States (contd.)

Operations In Virginia	Operations In Cen. South	Operations In Miss. Valley	Coastal & Western Operations
October 1863			
14th & 15th: Cavalry battle at Bristoe Station, VA *15th:* Engagement at McClean's Ford, VA *18th:* Engagement at Charleston, WV *19th:* Cavalry engagement at Buckland Mills, VA	*7th:* Cavalry fight at Farmington, TN; Cavalry fight at Blue Springs, TN *20th & 22nd:* Cavalry fights at Philadelphia, TN *28th & 29th:* Battle of Wauhatchie, near Chattanooga, TN	*15th to 18th:* CSA cavalry attacks at Canton, Brownsville, and Clinton, MS *25th:* Engagement at Pine Bluff, AR	
November 1863			
6th: Engagement at Droop Mtn., VA *7th:* Battle of Rappahannock Station, VA; engagement at Kelly's Ford, VA *26th to 30th:* Operations at Mine Run, VA, ending in retirement of Union army to north bank of Rapidan River	*7th:* Cavalry fight at Rogersville, TN *14th:* Cavalry fight at Huff's Ferry, TN *16th:* Engagement at Campbell's Station, TN *17th to Dec 4th:* Siege of Knoxville by Longstreet *23rd to 25th:* Bragg driven away from Chattanooga; Battles of Chattanooga, Lookout Mountain, Orchard Knob, Missionary Ridge *27th:* Rear-guard actions at Ringgold Gap and Taylor's Ridge, GA	*3rd:* Engagement at Grand Coteau, LA	*6th:* Brownsville, TX, occupied by Union troops *16th:* Corpus Christi, TX, occupied by Union troops

A Synoptic Table of Events in the War Between the States (contd.)

Operations In Virginia	Operations In Cen. South	Operations In Miss. Valley	Coastal & Western Operations
DECEMBER 1863			
7th: Confederate Congress meets *8th to 21st:* Averill's Union raid in southwestern VA	*2nd:* Cavalry skirmish at Walker's Ford, TN *10th to 14th:* Engagements at Bean's Station and Morristown, TN *28th:* Cavalry skirmish at Charlestown, TN	*1st to 4th:* Engagement at Ripley, Moscow, and Salisbury, TN	*30th:* Engagement at St. Augustine, FL
JANUARY 1864			
3rd: Cavalry engagement at Jonesville, VA *29th to Feb 1st:* Cavalry skirmishes at Medley, WV *31st:* Engagement at Smithfield, VA	*16th & 17th:* Engagement at Dandridge, TN *19th & 24th:* Engagements at Tazewell, TN *27th:* Engagement at Fair Gardens, or Kelly's Ford, TN		
FEBRUARY 1864			
3rd: Engagement at Morton's Ford, VA *17th:* Confederate Congress adjourns *28th to Mar. 4th:* Kilpatrick's and Dahlgren's raid on Richmond, VA	*25th to 27th:* Engagement at Buzzard Roost and Rocky Face, GA	*3rd to Mar. 5th:* Sherman's expedition from Vicksburg and Jackson to Meridian, MS *10th to 25th:* William Sooy Smith's cavalry expedition from Memphis to Meridian; driven back by Forrest	*1st to 3rd:* CSA attempt to retake New Bern, NC, unsuccessful *9th to 14th:* Union advances into interior Florida *17th:* CSA submarine *Hunley* sinks U.S.S. *Housatonic* off Charleston, SC *20th:* Union defeated at Oluston, FL

A Synoptic Table of Events in the War Between the States (contd.)

OPERATIONS IN VIRGINIA	OPERATIONS IN CEN. SOUTH	OPERATIONS IN MISS. VALLEY	COASTAL & WESTERN OPERATIONS
		MARCH 1864	
9th: **Grant made commander of all Union armies**	*9th:* **Sherman put into command in West**		
		14th: Union General Banks' Red River captures Ft. DeRussy, LA	
		24th: Union City, TN, and garrison captured by Forrest	
		25th: Forrest's raid, Paducah, KY	
		26th to 30th: Engagements at Long-view and Mt. Elba, AR	
		APRIL 1864	
		8th and 9th: Banks' Red River expe-dition defeated and turned-back at Pleasant Hill and Mansfield, LA	
		10th to 30th: Retreat of Steele's Union expedition to Little Rock, with engagements at Prairie D'Ann, 10th; Moscow, 13th; Liberty, 15th; Camden, 16th; Poison Springs, 18th; Mark's Mill, 26th; Jenkin's Ferry, 30th	
		12th: Forrest storms Ft. Pillow, TN	
		12th to 24th: Retreat of Banks' Expe-dition to New Orleans, with CSA attacks at Blair's Landing, 12th; Monetta's Ferry, 22nd; Cloutierville, 24th	
			17th to 20th: CSA troops and iron-clad *Albemarle* retake Plymouth, NC

A Synoptic Table of Events in the War Between the States (contd.)

Operations In Virginia	Operations In Cen. South	Operations In Miss. Valley	Coastal & Western Operations
MAY 1864			
2nd: Confederate Congress meets in Richmond, VA **5th to 7th: Battle of the Wilderness, VA** **8th:** Cavalry fight at Todd's Tavern, VA **8th to 18th: Battle of Spotsylvania Court House, VA,** including Bloody Angle **9th & 10th:** Engagement at Swift Creek, VA **9th to 25th:** Sheridan's Cavalry Raid on Richmond; including engagements at Beaver Dam Station, South Anna, Ashland **Yellow Tavern; CSA Maj. Gen. J.E.B. Stuart mortally wounded** **10th:** Engagement at Crockett's Cove, VA **12th to 16th:** Battle of Ft. Darling, on Drewry's Bluff, VA **15th:** Union forces defeated at Battle of New Market, VA **20th:** Battle of Bermuda Hundred; Butler "bottled up" **23rd to 28th:** Battles at North Anna and Totopotomoy Creek **27th & 28th:** Cavalry battles at: Hanovertown and Salem Church, VA **30th:** Cavalry engagement at Ashland, VA	**5th to 9th:** Opening of Sherman's campaign at Rocky Ford, GA **9th:** Cavalry fight at Varnell's Station, GA **13th to 16th:** Battle of Resaca, GA; engagements at Lay's or Turner's Ferry, GA **17th:** Skirmish at Adairsville, GA **18th:** Skirmish at Rome and Kingston, GA **19th to 22nd:** CSA stand at Caseville, GA **25th to June 4th:** Battles about Dallas, New Hope Church, and Pickett's Mill, GA **26th to 29th:** Cavalry engagements at Decatur and Moulton, GA	**1st to 8th:** Retreat of Bank's Red River expedition continued **5th:** Union gunboats at Dunn's Bayou attacked by Taylor **18th:** Engagement at Bayou de Glaize or Calhoun Station, LA	**5th:** CSA ram *Albemarle* engages Union fleet in Roanoke River, NC; CSA attempts to retake New Bern, NC, defeated Cruiser C.S.S. *Georgia* commissioned

A Synoptic Table of Events in the War Between the States (contd.)

Operations in Virginia	Operations in Cen. South	Operations in Miss. Valley	Coastal & Western Operations
June 1864			
1st to 3rd: Battle of Cold Harbor, VA *5th:* Battle of Piedmont, VA *10th & 11th:* Engagement at Lexington, VA *12th:* Cavalry battle of Trevillion's Station, VA *14th:* Confederate Congress adjourned *14th:* Grant begins crossing to south side of James River, VA *15rd to 19th:* Attacks on Petersburg, VA, met by Beauregard's force, reinforced by Lee on 18th **Siege of Petersburg begun, to last until April 2, 1865** *18th:* Hunter's army driven away from Lexington, VA *22nd to 30th:* Engagements on Jerusalem Plank Road and Weldon Railroad, Petersburg, VA	*9th:* Morgan's last raid into Kentucky surprised at Mt. Sterling *9th to 30th:* Kennesaw Mountain period of Sherman's campaign, including Pine Mountain, Gilgal Church, Big Shanty, and general assault on Kennesaw Mountain, 27th *10th:* Morgan captures Cynthania, KY *12th:* Morgan defeated at Cynthania, KY	*6th:* Engagement at Lake Chicot, AR *10th:* **Forrest routs Sturgis' invasion of Mississippi at Brice's Cross Roads, or Guntown, MS, near Tupelo**	*19th:* Cruiser C.S.S. *Alabama* sunk off Cherbourg, France, by U.S.S. *Kearsarge*
July 1864			
1st to 31st: Siege of Petersburg - Richmond continued *4th to 20th:* CSA Major General Early's raid on Washington, DC, including engagements about Harper's Ferry, 4th to 7th; Monocacy River, 9th; Ft. Stevens, 12th; Cavalry fights in Blue Ridge gaps and lower Valley 17th to 20th *23rd to 24th:* Third Battle of Kernstown and Winchester, VA *30th:* "Crater" mine exploded at Petersburg, VA	*2nd to 5th:* Union victory at Smyrna Station, GA *6th to 10th:* Sherman crosses Chattahoochee River, GA *18th:* Hood replaces Johnston in command of the Army of Tennessee *20th:* Battle of Peach Tree Creek, near Atlanta, GA *22nd:* **Battle of Atlanta, GA** *26th to 31st:* Stoneman's raid to Macon, GA *28th:* Battle of Ezra Church, GA *28th to Sept. 2nd:* Sherman's Siege of Atlanta, GA	*14th:* Battle of Tupelo, MS (or Harrisburg) *27th:* Engagement at Ft. Smith, AR	*5th to 7th:* Union land attack on Charleston, SC, defenses repulsed

A Synoptic Table of Events in the War Between the States (contd.)

Operations In Virginia	Operations In Cen. South	Operations In Miss. Valley	Coastal & Western Operations
		AUGUST 1864	
1st to 31st: Siege of Petersburg, VA, continues; engagements on Jerusalem Plank Road at Globe Tavern, and Ream's Station on the Weldon Railroad *1st to 31st:* Early remains in the lower valley, with engagements at White Post; Sulphur Springs Bridge; Berryville Pike; Snicker's Gap; Fisher's Hill; Front Royal; Winchester; Berryville; Halltown; Smithfield, VA	*1st to 31st:* Siege of Atlanta continues, with CSA cavalry raids on railroads to the rear *31st & Sept. 1st:* Battle of Jonesboro, Ga.	*21st:* Forrest's raid into Memphis, TN, to force recall of A. J. Smith's expedition from Mississippi	*5th:* Farragut's fleet enters Mobile Bay, captures CSA ram *Tennessee*; with army, captures Ft. Gaines *6th:* Cruiser C.S.S. *Tallahassee* leaves Wilmington, NC, for three-week cruise *17th:* Engagement at Gainesville, FL *23rd:* Union navy captures Ft. Morgan, FL
		SEPTEMBER 1864	
1st to 31st: Siege of Petersburg continued; Union attacks on 28th & 30th repulsed *1st to 18th:* Early remains in lower valley, with engagements at Berryville, Lock's Ford, and Sycamore Church, VA *19th:* Fourth Battle of Winchester, VA; Early driven-up valley *22nd:* Early defeated at Fisher's Hill, VA	*1st to 8th:* Wheeler's cavalry raid into Tennessee *2nd:* **Atlanta, GA, surrendered to Sherman** *4th:* CSA Col. J. H. Morgan killed at Greeneville, TN *21st to Oct. 6th:* Forrest's raid into Middle Tennessee	*1st to 20th:* CSA Gen. Sterling Price's expedition to Missouri *26th:* Engagement at Pilot Knob *27th:* Engagement at Centralia	*16th & 18th:* Skirmishes at Ft. Gibson, Indian Territory

A Synoptic Table of Events in the War Between the States (contd.)

OPERATIONS IN VIRGINIA	OPERATIONS IN CEN. SOUTH	OPERATIONS IN MISS. VALLEY	COASTAL & WESTERN OPERATIONS
OCTOBER 1864			
1st to 31st: Siege of Petersburg, VA, continues; Engagements at Darbytown Road, 7th & 13th; Hatcher's Run, 27th; Fair Oaks, 27th & 28th *2nd:* Union expedition to Saltville, VA, saltworks repulsed *9th:* Cavalry fight at Fisher's Hill *12th:* Cavalry fight at Strasburg, VA *19th:* Battle of Cedar Creek, VA	*1st to 15th:* Hood raids in-force against Sherman's communications with engagements at Big Shanty, Acworth, Allatoona Pass, Resaca, and Dalton, GA *22nd:* Hood starts on Tennessee Campaign	*1st to 28th:* Price remains in Missouri with engagements at Glasgow, Little Blue River, Big Blue River, Westport, and Newtonia	*7th:* Cruiser C.S.S. *Florida* sunk at Bahia, Brazil *8th:* Cruiser C.S.S. *Shenandoah* commissioned *27th:* CSA ram *Albemarle* destroyed at Plymouth, NC, by torpedo attack
NOVEMBER 1864			
1st to 30th: Siege of Petersburg continues. Early remains in Valley, with engagements at Newtown, Cedar Springs, Rood's Hill *7th:* Congress meets at Richmond	*4th:* Forrest's cavalry destroys Union base and boats at Johnsonville, TN *16th:* Hood crosses Tennessee River on Tennessee campaign; Sherman leaves Atlanta for March to the Sea *21st:* Georgia state troops defeated at Griswoldville, GA *26th:* Wheeler's cavalry's engagement at Sandersville, GA *29th:* Confederate attack at Spring Hill, TN, failed *30th:* Battle of Franklin, TN		*30th:* Engagement at Honey Hill, or Grahamsville, SC
DECEMBER 1864			
1st to 31st: Siege of Petersburg continues; with engagements at Stony Creek Station, Weldon Railroad, Hatcher's Run *8th to 28th:* Sheridan's raid on Gordonsville, VA *12th to 21st:* Union raid from Bean's Station, TN, to Virginia saltworks	*1st to 14th:* Hood's army in front of Nashville, TN *1st to 10th:* Sherman marches to Savannah, GA *7th:* Engagement at Murfreesboro, TN *10th to 21st:* Siege of Savannah, GA *13th:* Ft. McAllister, GA, captured by Sherman *15th and 16th:* Battle of Nashville, TN *21st:* Savannah, GA, evacuated	*26th:* Engagement at Egypt Station, MS	*6th & 9th:* Engagement at Devereaux's Neck, SC *25th:* Ft. Fisher, below Wilmington, NC, repulses Union land and naval expedition
JANUARY 1865			
1st to 31st: Siege of Petersburg continues			*15th:* Ft. Fisher captured *30th:* Cruiser C.S.S. *Stonewall* commissioned

A Synoptic Table of Events in the War Between the States (contd.)

OPERATIONS IN VIRGINIA	OPERATIONS IN CEN. SOUTH	OPERATIONS IN MISS. VALLEY	COASTAL & WESTERN OPERATIONS
FEBRUARY 1865			
1st to 28th: Siege of Petersburg continues, with engagements at Dabney's Mills, 5th to 7th *3rd:* Hampton Roads "Peace Conference" fails *6th:* Lee made commander-in-chief *27th to March 25th:* Sheridan's raid in Virginia	*1st:* Sherman starts north from Savannah, GA *17th:* Columbia, SC, taken and burned; Charleston evacuated	 *22nd:* Engagement at Douglas Landing, Pine Bluff, AR	 *22nd:* Wilmington, NC, captured
MARCH 1865			
1st to 31st: Siege of Petersburg continues, with engagements at Ft. Stedman, 25th; Quaker Road, 29th; Boydton Plank & White Oak Roads, and Dinwiddie Courthouse, 31st *2nd:* Early's command dispersed or captured by Sheridan at Waynesboro, VA *18th:* Confederate Congress adjourns *20th to April 6th:* Stoneman's raid from Tennessee	*10th:* Fayetteville, NC, and arsenal captured *16th:* Engagement at Averysboro, NC *19th to 21st:* Battle of Bentonville, NC	*22nd to April 24th:* Wilson's Union cavalry raid from Tenn. River to Selma, Montgomery, Columbus and Macon	*26th to April 12th:* Siege of Mobile, AL
APRIL 1865			
1st: Battle of Five Forks, VA *2nd:* Petersburg and Richmond evacuated *2nd to 9th:* Lee's army marches from Petersburg and Richmond to Appomattox Court House, with engagements at Amelia Springs, Sailor's Creek, High Bridge, Farmville and Appomattox *9th: Army of Northern Virginia surrendered at Appomattox Court House*	*2nd:* Wilson captures Selma, AL *13th:* Montgomery, AL, captured *16th:* Last engagement east of Mississippi at West Point, GA; Columbus, GA, taken *26th: Army of Tennessee surrendered at Greensboro, NC*		*22nd:* Mobile, AL, surrendered

A Synoptic Table of Events in the War Between the States (contd.)

Operations In Virginia	Operations In Cen. South	Operations In Miss. Valley	Coastal & Western Operations
		MAY 1865	
	4th: Department of Alabama, Mississippi and East Louisiana surrendered *10th:* President Davis captured at Irwinsville, GA	*11th:* Troops in Arkansas surrendered at Chalk Bluff	*11th:* Troops in Florida surrendered at Tallahassee *13th:* **Last land engagement of war at Palmetto Ranch, near Brownsville, TX** *15th:* Cruiser C.S.S. *Stonewall* surrendered *26th:* Army of Trans-Mississippi Department surrendered
		JUNE 1865	
			2nd: Galveston, TX, surrendered *28th:* **Cruiser C.S.S. *Shenandoah* fires last shot of war in North Pacific**

Notes

1. Val C. Giles, "The Flag of the First Texas, A.N. Virginia," *Confederate Veteran*, Vol. 15, No. 9 (Sept. 1907).

2. *Public Ledger*, Philadelphia, Pennsylvania, Friday, October 17, 1862, Vol. 54, No. 23, front page.

3. Giles, "The Flag of the First Texas."

4. Howard M. Madaus, "The Southern Cross," an unpublished three-volume manuscript to be released for publication in the mid-1990s.

5. All information concerning this flag is courtesy of Howard Michael Madaus, "The Southern Cross." This anticipated three-volume set will prove to be the definitive reference work for battle flags of the entire Confederate Army.

6. *The Athens Daily Review*, Athens, Texas, society page, December 17, 1940.

7. *The Dallas News*, Dallas, Texas, May 18, 1961.

8. J. B. Polley, "Flags of the Fifth Texas Regiment, C.S.A," *Historical Reminiscences*. From an unknown vintage periodical, collection of the Daughters of the Republic of Texas at the Alamo, San Antonio, Texas.

9. *Ibid.*

10. *Ibid.*

11. Illustrations from data provided courtesy of the Colonel Harold B. Simpson Confederate Research Center, Hill College, Hillsboro, Texas, and Howard Madaus' "The Southern Cross."

12. J. B. Polley, "Flags of the Fifth Texas Regiment, C.S.A."

13. *Ibid.*

14. *Ibid.*

15. *Ibid.*

16. "The History of a Flag"; an unidentified but authoritative vintage newspaper article courtesy of the Colonel Harold B. Simpson Confederate Research Center, Hill College, Hillsboro, Texas.

17. Madaus, "The Southern Cross."

18. J. B. Polley, "Flags of the Fifth Texas Regiment, C.S.A."

19. *Ibid.*

20. Madaus, "The Southern Cross."

21. All information concerning this flag is derived from Madaus, "The Southern Cross."

22. Information concerning this flag provided by the Colonel Harold B. Simpson Confederate Research Center, Hill College, Hillsboro, Texas.

23. Unconfirmed source, supplied to aid in future research.

24. Source: Howard Michael Madaus, author of several publications listed in the bibliography of this text.

25. All information concerning this flag is from Madaus, "The Southern Cross."

26. *Ibid.*

27. *Ibid.*

28. *Ibid.*

29. Information on this flag provided by the Colonel Harold B. Simpson Confederate Research Center, Hill College, Hillsboro, Texas, and Madaus, "The Southern Cross." Photographs provided by the UDC–Texas.

30. Casual conversation with Kerry Hellums, New Mexico artist and recognized authority on Terry's Texas Rangers. The Colonel Harold B. Simpson Confederate Research Center, Hill College, Hillsboro, Texas, has the addresses and telephone numbers of several such authorities who have assumed the responsibilites of preserving and/or re-creating our Texas Confederate heritage.

31. Conversation with author/historian Charles Spurlin, who had heard this opinion from an elderly individual many years ago.

32. Report of the Adjutant-General of the State of Illinois (Springfield: H. W. Rokker, 1886), 2:614.

33. All information on this flag was derived from Madaus, "The Southern Cross."

34. All information concerning this flag courtesy Madaus, "The Southern Cross." Mr. Madaus initially surmised that a Van Dorn Pattern Flag had been captured from the Ninth Texas Cavalry at Corinth. He has since retracted that contention after his personal research confirmed otherwise. This position is supported by the fact that the surviving Ninth Texas Van Dorn flag was never captured.

35. *The Chicago Tribune*, November 4, 1863, erroneously refers to this flag as belonging to the "Sixth Texas Cavalry," an easy assumption with the number of dismounted cavalry serving as infantry at Arkansas Post.

36. *Official Records*, Series 1, Vol. 17, Pt. 1:708.

37. From information recorded at the Lycoming County Historical Society Museum, Williamsport, Virginia, when this flag was donated to the Society by a member of the Reno G.A.R. Post, a former soldier in the Fifteenth Regiment, Missouri Volunteer Infantry, U.S.A.

38. *Official Records*, Vol. 17, Pt. 1:727.

39. Source: Colonel Harold B. Simpson Confederate Research Center, Hill College, Hillsboro, Texas.

40. All information on this flag from Madaus, "The Southern Cross." Mr. Madaus has identified many flags that are in private collections.

41. *Official Records*, Series 1, Vol. 15:1032–1033.

42. All information concerning this flag from Madaus, "The Southern Cross."

43. From the memoirs of F. G. Crawford, in possession of the Crawford family. Account provided by Don Crawford, Victoria, TX. F. G. Crawford served in the Thirty-second (a.k.a. Thirty-sixth) Texas Cavalry, Trans-Mississippi theater.

44. From a photograph in the collection of Don Crawford, Victoria, TX.

45. June Tuck, *Civil War Shadows in Hopkins County*. Mrs. Tuck has noted a vintage letter revealing that Kate Ashburn and Fannie Becton presented this flag to the brigade's first reunion. It was donated to Texas A&M University in 1927. This probably is true, as the regiments in Ross' Brigade are known to have used St. Andrew's Cross type variants in early 1864. The fact that brigades, as combined regiments, were not issued flags during the war strengthens the contention that A&M's "Ross' Brigade" flag was a postwar ceremonial color. An illustration of a regimental "Cameron Flag" as used in Ross' Brigade in 1864 is provided in this text as the regimental color of the Third Texas Cavalry.

46. Information concerning this flag from Madaus, "The Southern Cross." This flag has been noted in at least one other reference.

47. All information concerning this flag from Madaus, "The Southern Cross."

48. *Ibid.*

49. *Ibid.*

50. *Ibid.*

51. *Confederate Veteran*, Vol. 7, No. 12 (December 1899): 545–546.

52. C. C. Jefferies, *Terry's Texas Rangers* (New York: Vantage Press, 1961), 100.

53. *Report of the Adjutant General of the State of Indiana* (Indianapolis, Indiana, Alexander Conner, 1865–1868), Vol. 1, Appendix, 170 (Document No. 23).

54. Jefferies, *Terry's Texas Rangers.*

55. The frustration concerning the unavailability of this unique flag is overwhelming. The author has failed to locate a single photo of this flag.

56. All information concerning this flag from Madaus, "The Southern Cross."

57. *Confederate Veteran*, Vol. 7, No. 12 (December 1899): 545–546.

58. *Official Records*, Series I, Vol. 39, Pt. 1:727.

59. Information concerning this flag from Madaus, "The Southern Cross."

60. *Ibid.*

61. Association with this unit has been suggested by Howard M. Madaus, author of *The Battle Flags of the Confederate Army of Tennessee* and "The Southern Cross."

62. Information concerning this flag from Madaus, "The Southern Cross."

63. *Ibid.*

64. *Official Records*, Series I, Vol. 49, Pt. 1:269, Pt. 2:336.

65. Information concerning this flag from Madaus, "The Southern Cross."

66. *Confederate Veteran*, Vol. 36, No. 2 (February 1928): 50.

67. Information concerning this flag from Madaus, "The Southern Cross."

68. *Ibid.*

69. Register of Captured Flags, 1861–1865, Records of the Adjutant-General's Office (Record Group No. 94), National Archives, Washington, D.C.

Bibliography

Printed Sources

Battles and Leaders of the Civil War. New York: Castle Books, 1956.

Brown, Norman D. *One of Cleburne's Command*. Austin: University of Texas Press.

Cannon, Devereaux, Jr. *The Flags of the Confederacy*. St. Luke's Press, 1988.

Chance, Joseph E. *The Second Texas Infantry*. Austin: Eakin Press, 1984.

Civil War Diary of Charles A. Leuschner. Austin: Eakin Press, 1992.

Confederate Battle Flags: In the Collection of the Old State House, A Museum of Arkansas History. Little Rock: Old State House Arkansas Commemorative Commission, 1988.

Crute, Joseph H., Jr. *Emblems of Southern Valor: The Battle Flags of the Confederacy*. Louisville, KY.

——. *Units of the Confederate States Army*. Derwent Books, 1987.

Davis, William. *Battlefields of the Civil War*. Smithmark Publishing, 1991.

Echoes of Glory: Arms and Equipment of the Confederacy. Time-Life Books, 1991.

Grimes, Roy, ed. *300 Years in Victoria*. Victoria Advocate Publishing Co., 1968.

Henry, Ralph Selph. *The Story of the Confederacy*. Indianapolis, IN: Bobbs-Merrill Co., 1931. Reprinted 1989 by Del Capo Publishing, New York.

Jones, Tom. *Hood's Texas Brigade Sketchbook*. Hillsboro, TX: Hill College Press, 1988.

Katcher, Philip, and Rick Scollins. *Flags of the American Civil War: Vol. 1 Confederate*. Osprey Publications, 1992.

Kerr, Homer. *Fighting with Ross' Cavalry Brigade*. Hill Junior College Press.

Madaus, Howard M. "The Southern Cross." 3-vol. Unpublished manuscript.

Madaus, Howard M., and Robert Needham. *Unit Colors of the Trans-Mississippi Confederacy*. Parts I–III. Washington, DC: 1989.

——. *Battle Flags of the Confederate Army of Tennessee*. Milwaukee Public Museum, 1976.

Pratt, Fletcher. *Civil War in Pictures*. Garden City Publishers, 1954.

Simpson, Col. Harold B. *Hood's Texas Brigade: Lee's Grenadier Guard*. Waco: Texian Press, 1970.

Smith, Ralph J. *Reminiscences of the Civil War*. W. M. Morrison, Publ., 1962.

Thompson, Jerry Don. *Vaqueros in Blue and Gray*. Austin: Presidial, 1976.

Tuck, June E. *Civil War Shadows in Hopkins County*. Sulphur Springs, TX.

Walter, John, comp. *Confederate Unit Histories*. Middle Village, NY. From official records and correspondence of Civil War soldiers.

Ware, Charles E. *The Returned Battle Flags*. St. Louis, MO: 1905.

Wright, Mrs. D. Giraud (Louise Wigfall). *A Southern Girl in '61: The War-time Memories of a Confederate Senator's Daughter*. NY: Doubleday, Page & Co., 1905.

Museums and Archival Collections

Chicago Historical Society, Chicago IL

Colonel Harold B. Simpson Confederate Research Center, Hill College, Hillsboro, TX

Confederate Memorial Hall, New Orleans, LA

Harrison County Museum, Marshall, TX

Library of the Daughters of the Texas Revolution, Alamo, San Antonio, TX

Museum of the Confederacy, Richmond, VA

New Market Battlefield Military Museum, New Market, VA

Old State House Museum, Little Rock, AR

Rosenberg Library, Galveston, TX

Sam Houston Regional Library and Research Center, Liberty, TX

Smith County Historical Society, Tyler, TX

Sons of Confederate Veterans, Trans-Mississippi Division
Terrell Heritage Museum, Terrell, TX
Texas National Guard Museum, Camp Mabry, Austin, TX
Texas State Archives, Austin, TX
United Daughters of the Confederacy–Texas Division, Austin, TX
Victoria College, Victoria, TX

Acknowledgments

The author would like to acknowledge the special assistance and talents of Howard Michael Madaus, Cody, Wyoming; Dr. B. D. Patterson and Ms. Peggy Fox, Colonel Harold B. Simpson Confederate Research Center, Hill College, Hillsboro, Texas; and William I. Thornton, Richardson, Texas.

Index